ACHIEVING
EYPS

Supporting Pedagogy and Practice in Early Years Settings

3.2011

ACHIEVING
EYPS

Supporting Pedagogy and Practice in Early Years Settings

SHIRLEY F. ALLEN

MARY E. WHALLEY

Series editors: Gill Goodliff and Lyn Trodd

LearningMatters

First published in 2010 by Learning Matters Ltd

All rights reserved. No part of this publication may be reproduced, stored in a retrieval system or transmitted in any form by any means, electronic, mechanical, photocopying, recording, or otherwise, without prior permission in writing from Learning Matters Ltd.

© 2010 Copyright Shirley F. Allen and Mary E. Whalley

British Library Cataloguing in Publication Data
A CIP record for this book is available from the British Library.

ISBN: 978 1 84445 465 5

This book is also available in the following ebook formats:

Adobe ebook   ISBN: 978 1 84445 705 2
EPUB ebook   ISBN: 978 1 84445 704 5
Kindle   ISBN: 978 1 84445 993 3

The right of Shirley F. Allen and Mary E. Whalley to be identified as the Authors of this work has been asserted by them in accordance with the Copyright, Design and Patents Act 1988.

Cover design by Phil Barker
Text design by Code 5 Design Associates Ltd
Project management by Swales & Willis Ltd, Exeter, Devon
Typeset by Swales & Willis Ltd, Exeter, Devon
Printed and bound in Great Britain by TJ International Ltd, Padstow, Cornwall

Learning Matters Ltd
33 Southernhay East
Exeter EX1 1NX
Tel: 01392 215560
info@learningmatters.co.uk
www.learningmatters.co.uk

FSC
Mixed Sources
Product group from well-managed
forests and other controlled sources
Cert no. SGS-COC-2482
www.fsc.org
© 1996 Forest Stewardship Council

Contents

Foreword from the series editors   vii

About the authors and series editors   ix

Acknowledgements   x

1   Introduction   1

2   Perspectives on Early Years pedagogy   13

3   Children's learning and development   29

4   Meeting the needs of all children   45

5   A safe and stimulating environment   66

6   The role of the EYP in supporting children's learning   83

7   Sustained shared thinking   98

8   Evaluating effective practice   114

9   Continuing professional development   131

Appendix 1: Piaget's stages of cognitive development   146

Appendix 2: Further Piagetian concepts   147

References   148

Index   160

Foreword from the series editors

This book is one of a series that will be of interest to anyone following one of the pathways towards achieving Early Years Professional Status (EYPS). This includes students on Sector-Endorsed Foundation Degree in Early Years programmes and undergraduate Early Childhood Studies degree courses, as these awards are key routes towards EYPS.

The graduate EYP role was created as a key strategy in government commitment to improve the quality of Early Years care and education in England, especially in the private, voluntary and independent sectors. Policy documents and legislation such as *Every Child Matters: Change for Children* (DfES, 2004), the *Ten Year Childcare Strategy: Choice for Parents – the Best Start for Children* (HMT, 2004) and the Childcare Act 2006, identified the need for high-quality, well-trained and educated professionals to work with the youngest children. The government's aim – restated in the *Statutory Framework for the Early Years Foundation Stage* (DCSF, 2008a) – is to have an Early Years Professional (EYP) in all children's centres by 2010 and in every full day care setting by 2015, with two graduates in disadvantaged areas.

In *Supporting Pedagogy and Practice in Early Years Settings*, Mary Whalley and Shirley Allen focus on the group of EYP Standards clustered under the heading 'Effective Practice' (CWDC, 2008). They highlight how the Early Years Professional role is key to enhancing the effectiveness of practice within the Early Years Foundation Stage (EYFS) and to the government's agenda to improve outcomes for children.

The authors explore the role of the pedagogue and its potential as a model for the EYP in leading delivery of the EYFS Framework, and encourage the reader to engage in a critical reflection of the concepts of 'effectiveness' and 'high quality' in the context of pedagogy and practice in the Early Years. Drawing on theory and key research studies to discuss a range of approaches and perspectives that inform, and influence, contemporary understanding of pedagogy in the Early Years, each chapter examines facets of effective practice.

Through reflective and practical tasks the reader is challenged to engage with different aspects of pedagogy and to set these in the practical context of planning for children's learning and development within an enabling environment. Case studies and self-assessment questions, linked to meeting the EYP Standards, prompt reflection on how the EYP demonstrates effective practice and leads and supports the practice of others. The opportunities afforded by EYP Networks in offering post-validation support and ongoing opportunities for study and learning are considered, and EYPs are encouraged to continue their participation in a 'community of learners' with a commitment to exploring options for continuing professional development.

July 2010

Gill Goodliff   Lyn Trodd
The Open University   University of Hertfordshire

About the authors and series editors

Shirley F. Allen

Shirley Allen is a Senior Lecturer in Early Childhood Studies at Middlesex University, where she has been Co-Leader of the Early Years Professional Status programme since the Pilot Phase in 2006, and also works on the Early Childhood Studies degree. Previously, Shirley worked at the University of Hertfordshire on teacher education programmes and was an Early Years teacher in London schools for many years before moving into higher education.

Mary E. Whalley

Mary Whalley worked as a school teacher in Reception and Early Years classes for a number of years, including a post as Teacher Fellow at the University of Manchester. More recently, Mary has taught at Leeds Metropolitan University and at Harrogate College on both the Foundation Degree Early Years and BA Childhood Studies degree. She combines her role in teaching with that of EYPS tutor and assessor. Her greatest teachers remain her own children and grandchildren.

Gill Goodliff

Gill Goodliff is a Senior Lecturer and Head of Awards for Early Years at the Open University where she has developed and chaired courses on the Sector Endorsed Foundation Degree and as a Lead Assessor for Early Years Professional Status. Her professional work with young children and their families was predominantly in the voluntary sector. Her research interests centre on the professional identities of Early Years practitioners and young children's spirituality.

Lyn Trodd

Lyn Trodd is Head of Children's Workforce Development at the University of Hertfordshire. She is the Chair of the National Network of Sector-Endorsed Foundation Degrees in Early Years. She was involved in the design of Early Years Professional Status and helped to pilot the Validation Pathway when it first became available. Lyn has published and edited a range of articles, national and international conference papers and books focusing on self-efficacy in the child and the practitioner, and also the professional identity and role of adults who work with young children.

Acknowledgements

The authors wish to express thanks to a number of people without whom this book would not have been written. Gill Goodliff, the lead editor in this book in the *Achieving EYPS* series, has offered us unstinting support throughout the writing and her feedback and encouragement have been invaluable.

It has been a joy to work with the team at Learning Matters and our special thanks must be recorded to Julia Morris, Amy Thornton and Jennifer Clark for their patience and efficiency in responding to all our requests and queries and believing that this book would, indeed, see publication!

The book could not have been written without a group of EYPs from across the country who willingly shared their experiences and practices with us. We believe it is these 'stories from practice' which form the core of the book and we are so grateful to all those busy EYPs and aspiring EYPs who took the time to step back and reflect on their own pedagogical base and share their reflections with us for inclusion in the book.

Our families are utterly deserving of our gratitude, too, for their backing, love and understanding, so special thanks from Mary to Ernie, Sara, Rachel, Nia and James; and from Shirley to Michael, Chris and Nick. We could not have met the deadlines without you!

Finally – we want to thank each other! We only managed to meet up face-to-face occasionally but have worked very closely together throughout the process, bouncing ideas off and occasionally challenging each other. We believe our effective collaboration here models something of the teamwork that is a key feature of Early Years practice today.

Mary E. Whalley
Shirley F. Allen

July 2010

1   Introduction

CHAPTER OBJECTIVES

This chapter provides a rationale for the book and introduces the key themes to be addressed within it. 'Effectiveness' within Early Years practice, particularly in the delivery of the Early Years Foundation Stage (EYFS) Statutory Framework (DCSF, 2008a) is the central theme. Definitions of Early Years pedagogy are offered within the contemporary context in England and the role of Early Years Professional (EYP) is discussed alongside concepts of 'effectiveness' and 'quality practice'. Reflective tasks are included to support the gathering of evidence required to achieve Early Years Professional Status.

After reading this chapter you should be able to:
- critically appraise the role of the pedagogue and its potential as a model for the role of Early Years Professional in leading delivery of the Early Years Foundation Stage Framework;
- explore concepts of 'effectiveness' and 'high quality' in the context of Early Years pedagogy and practice;
- begin to apply an understanding of the Early Years Professional Standards to your own role and practice.

Introduction

The role of Early Years Professional is fundamental to the government's agenda to develop *high quality leadership and a high quality workforce . . . [which are] essential for children to get the best possible start from Early Years provision* (DCSF, 2008b, p111) Candidates seeking validation for Early Years Professional Status (EYPS) are required to demonstrate that they can meet all 39 Standards through their own personal practice, and also provide evidence that they can lead and support others to do so (CWDC, 2008). This chapter introduces the themes to be addressed in the book and will help you to reflect on your understanding of Early Years pedagogy; it has broad relevance to most of the EYP Standards.

What do we mean by 'effectiveness' in EYFS delivery?

This book focuses on practice in the Early Years Foundation Stage (EYFS) and, in particular, what constitutes *effective* practice. The intention is that EYPs will model the skills and behaviours that promote good outcomes for children, and support and mentor other practitioners in doing so (CWDC, 2009a). The new understanding of Early Years leadership that is embedded in the EYP role has been explored previously (Whalley *et al.*, 2008) and applies directly to supporting effective practice. As an EYP, you will demonstrate:

- reflective and reflexive practice in your own role;

- skills in decision making;

- sound knowledge and understanding of Early Years pedagogy – the holistic needs of all children from birth to five and competence in planning, implementing and monitoring within the framework of the Early Years Foundation Stage framework (DCSF, 2008a);

- strong values of the intrinsic worth of each child and all those in her/his world;

- the ability to role model, lead and support others in high-quality practice;

- the ability to define a vision for practice within a setting;

- competence as an agent of change.

(Whalley *et al.*, 2008, p13)

Indeed, the government recognises that leadership is crucial to effectiveness through its stated commitment to *strengthening leadership for learning* in the Early Years – focusing on the key role of leaders in *building capacity and ensuring high quality learning and development* (DCSF, 2008c, p6) This book, then, aims to focus on the challenges and opportunities faced by EYPs in ensuring effective delivery of the EYFS. This assumes an understanding of Early Years pedagogy.

The focus of this book is EYP Standards 7–24, which are clustered under the heading 'Effective Practice' (CWDC, 2008), and encompass planning, resourcing, enabling and assessing learning within the EYFS for all the children in the setting:

> This group of Standards . . . describes the different facets of EYPs' practice that promote all children's well-being, and support and extend their learning and development.
>
> (CWDC, 2008: 21)

In this group of Standards, a number of aspects of 'effectiveness' are described that are interrelated and link equally to the requirements of the EYFS (DCSF, 2008a). These include values held by practitioners about the children for whom they are responsible and the expectations they have for them (S7); commitment to a safe, stimulating and accessible environment (S8, 17, 19, 20); provision for equality of opportunity (S12, 18); planning and provision of learning experiences (S9, 11, 12, 14, 15 and 16); differentiating provision to meet individual needs (S13, 23); and reviewing and evaluating children's well-being, learning and development (S10, 21, 22 and 24) (based on CWDC, 2008, p22). Each of these facets of 'effective practice' is explored more fully in this book. Reflective tasks and practical tasks are included in each chapter to encourage your engagement with the different aspects of pedagogy covered.

Within the EYFS documentation, you will find a number of direct references to 'effective practice' and 'quality provision'. In the Practice Guidance Sections 1.23–1.29 (DCSF, 2008d) there is a helpful focus on quality improvement, which is characterised by strong, well-qualified leadership promoting inclusive, personalised practice within a safe and stimulating environment. The concept of 'quality' is addressed a little later. The Principles into Practice (PiP) Cards (DCSF, 2008e) also include references to 'effective practice' that affirm the fundamental beliefs that underpin good Early Years practice. The CD-ROM that accompanies the EYFS pack (DCSF, 2008f) is a rich resource indeed. Make sure you access the additional documentation on 'effective practice' provided within this, as this offers valuable supporting guidance for you in building your evidence against the EYP Standards.

PRACTICAL TASK

Search for the following 'Effective Practice' documents on the EYFS CD-ROM under 'Resources' (DCFS, 2008e) and then match them to the relevant EYPS Standards in the table below.

CD-ROM	EYP Standards
Child Development: Effective Practice	
Health and Safety: Effective Practice	
Inclusive Practice: Effective Practice	
Keeping Safe: Effective Practice	
Key Person: Effective Practice	
Parents as Partners: Effective Practice	
Respecting Each Other: Effective Practice	
Supporting Learning: Effective Practice	
Outdoor Learning: Effective Practice	
The Wider Context: Effective Practice	
Multi-agency Working: Effective Practice	
Creativity and Critical Thinking: Effective Practice	
Play and Exploration: Effective Practice	

Contemporary understanding of Early Years pedagogy

The title for this book did not come readily or easily to the authors. Early Years pedagogy and the role of 'pedagogue' are not words yet in common parlance among practitioners across the majority of Early Years settings. Yet, these are important concepts that have direct relevance to the EYP role and ultimately to the child's experience within the EYFS. 'Pedagogy' (the art or science of teaching) is, at root, a Greek word meaning 'to lead the child'. McShane (2007, p1) reflects on the implications of this and suggests that the educational process, therefore, is about *supporting, walking beside and leading the child.* Such imagery is particularly apt for Early Years practice.

Two studies have broadened contemporary understanding of pedagogy within Early Years practice and provision. The outcomes of the Study of Pedagogical Effectiveness in Early Learning (SPEEL), (Moyles *et al.*, 2002a) and Researching Effective Pedagogy in the Early Years (Siraj-Blatchford *et al.*, 2002a) have been highly influential in the development of EYPS. There is opportunity to reflect further on the findings of the SPEEL and REPEY reports in Chapter 2, and to engage with the concept of the role of 'social pedagogue', commonly used in parts of Scandinavia, with which the EYP role bears comparison.

Stewart and Pugh (2007) suggest that Early Years pedagogy is:

> . . . *the understanding of how children learn and develop, and the practices through which we can enhance that process. It is rooted in values and beliefs about what we want for children, and supported by knowledge, theory and experience.*
>
> (Stewart and Pugh, 2007, cited in DCSF, 2009a, p4)

REFLECTIVE TASK

Begin to think about your understanding of 'pedagogy' and use the definition above to reflect on how you view your role as an EYP.

In the next chapter, findings from key national and international research studies are presented to provide the theoretical background to – and empirical evidence for – contemporary understanding of effective pedagogy in the Early Years. There are also reflective tasks to help you see the significance of these for your own role as an EYP.

Children's learning and development

Over the past decade or so, there has been an almost constant stream of high-quality writing about young children's learning and development (DCSF, 2009b). Contemporary Early Years practice is indebted to a range of writers who have highlighted the unique significance of the first five years of a child's life and of providing theoretical underpinning for provision for young children. One of the EYFS themes focuses on 'Learning and Development', acknowledging the interconnectedness of these, affirming the key commitments to play-based learning, to children learning actively through physical and mental challenges – including the opportunity to discover connections, and to think critically and ask questions (DCFS, 2008d, 4.1, 4.2, 4.3). Growing understanding of the place of schemas – *a pattern of repeatable behaviour into which experiences are assimilated and that are gradually coordinated* (Athey, 2007, p38) – in early childhood learning and development has been hugely significant in effective practice, and provides a clear window for practitioners to observe *how* young children learn.

Standard 2 relates to the EYPs' *detailed knowledge and understanding of the broad developmental stages of children from birth to the end of the EYFS* (CWDC, 2008, p15) and is based on the premise that young children are competent learners from birth. So it is important that, as EYPs, you are knowledgeable about normative development from birth to five (and beyond), and about the major supporting theories that underpin this. Equally, it is important that you have a clear grasp that there are significant factors that can affect development: biological, social, cultural and environmental. You will also be required to demonstrate your understanding that children develop at different speeds in different competencies and that you can take account of children who experience developmental delay or who develop in a different way.

In Chapter 3, in particular, the place of play in early learning and development is examined. Few practitioners would question that play and exploration have a central role in early childhood and this is supported by a wealth of research (e.g. Broadhead, 2004; Wood and Atfield, 2005; Broadhead, Howard and Wood, 2010). Indeed, play is a fundamental commitment within the EYFS (DCSF, 2009a). But, what does 'learning through play' really mean? What does it look like in practice? And – as EYPs – what is your role in enabling, supporting and resourcing playful learning? Closely linked to these aspects of the EYP role are those of observing, listening to and assessing children's learning, especially as they are engaged in purposeful play. Observation can be a valuable tool in collecting information about children from their play. It is in play-based assessments that staff can observe not only what children can do and what different skills they have acquired, but how they are using those skills (Palaiologou, 2008). Because play is a child's natural and – usually – spontaneous behaviour, and given the unthreatening nature of play, children will often demonstrate the best of their abilities in play contexts (Sayeed and Guerin, 2000).

Standard 27 focuses on listening to children. Increasingly, Early Years practitioners are using the Mosaic Approach (Clark and Moss, 2005) to show that they value children's views and perspectives. This was developed as a result of *a search . . . for a way to listen to young children [talking] about their own lives* (Clark and Moss, 2005, p12). It offers a multi-method framework for listening to children and, while the initial study was carried out at the Thomas Coram Research Institute in London, it draws significantly on the work of the Reggio Emilia pre-schools in Italy and the 'Hundred Languages of Children' described by Malaguzzi (in Edwards *et al.*, 1998). In Chapter 3, you have opportunity to reflect in more detail on how you might develop skills in observing and listening to children, but take a moment here to pause.

Equality and diversity

Within the EYFS, the first-listed theme is that of the 'Unique Child', which acknowledges that each child in any group will be developing in a unique way, with individual interests, communication and learning styles. As an EYP, you will be instrumental in supporting each child's development and learning, affirming each with equal value and respect. This includes having high expectations of each *becoming all that (s/he) is capable of becoming* (Maslow, 1999). Look again at Standard 7 and see how this aspect of the EYP role is captured here.

In Chapter 4, we discuss what it means to lead equality practice. As EYPs, you have a professional responsibility for understanding something of our own social history, of key changes in law, and the impact of both these on shaping and informing contemporary Early Years practice. Fundamentally, this includes strong partnerships with families and communities, where no child or family is discriminated against. Lindon (2006, p3) describes this as *equalising opportunities for those children and families whose situation or group identity may place them at a disadvantage*.

The EYFS quite clearly sets out the responsibilities for providers of equality practice (DCSF, 2008a). These not only require that positive attitudes to diversity and difference are nurtured but that children *from their earliest age [learn] to value diversity in others and grow up making a positive contribution to society* (DCSF, 2008a, 1.14). This lofty rhetoric offers a significant mix of opportunities and challenges. Indeed, within the EYFS documentation (DCSF, 2008d, 1.1), a pertinent question is put to practitioners: *How [can we] meet the differing and competing needs of every child, while being 'fair' about time spent with individual children [who most need it]?*

This book provides you with exercises and tasks designed to help you to identify and reflect on how you demonstrate effective practice, and lead the practice of others, in meeting the needs of boys and girls, children from different kinds of families, those with different religious beliefs and from different cultural backgrounds, and those who have specific medical, physical or learning needs – including those who are very able.

A safe and stimulating environment

A further theme in the EYFS is that of the 'Enabling Environment' and, in Chapter 5, a number of key issues relating to the setting's provision are addressed. This includes consideration of the physical environment and resources that encourage challenge, the way the environment is planned and how children's well-being is nurtured. In this chapter, too, there is important reference to new technologies that support learning and development.

Standards 8, 9, 11, 12 and 19 focus specifically on the role of the EYP in providing this 'Enabling Environment'. Young children need the *confidence to explore and learn in safe, secure and yet challenging indoor and outdoor spaces* (DCSF, 2008d, 3.3) and, for the EYP, this includes careful attention to the indoor, outdoor and emotional environment. DCSF (2008b) asks some important questions of practitioners/settings in respect of the effectiveness of the learning environment, as follows (adapted from DCSF, 2008b, p11).

- How are individual needs being recognised and met?
- How secure are practitioners in observing children's use of the learning environment/ resources (and carrying out changes as a result)?
- How often are resources checked for safety and quality?
- How do children choose their own resources for play?
- How are children involved in designing play environments?
- Does the environment look exciting from children's eye level?

The EYFS emphasises the importance of the emotional environment, recognising that it is 'created by all the people in the setting' (DCSF, 2008d, 3.3). It is only relatively recently that the importance of the emotional environment in supporting young children's well-being has been noted. The work of Goleman (1996) on 'emotional intelligence' is seminal here and children's social and emotional well-being is highlighted now as an essential concern for all who work with children (DfES, 2004 ff). One further question, explored in chapter 5, has particular relevance for the EYP:

> *How do setting leaders . . . monitor practitioners' modelling of behaviours to ensure children's well-being?*

The role of the adult in children's learning

We have now introduced three of the four 'themes' of the EYFS and the final one is 'Positive Relationships', which has relevance in any discussion on the role of the adult in effectively supporting children's learning. Debate continues about the adult role – especially in knowing how and when to get involved in children's play. In Chapter 6, the concept of a balanced approach is explored – with the differences between adult-initiated, adult-supported, adult-led and child-initiated learning examined and evaluated in the light of 'effective practice'.

However, in the definition of Early Years pedagogy that was offered earlier, the interactional and relational nature of learning and teaching was stressed. The growth of the Key Person approach proffered by Elfer *et al.* (2003) is rooted in an informed application of Bowlby's attachment theory (1988) and is now enshrined in the statutory requirements for EYFS provision (DCSF, 2008a). A well-managed Key Person approach is critical to effective practice for babies and very young children, and continues to have enormous benefits for children between three and five years, too. When it works well, the Key Person relationship ensures that a genuine bond is established with the individual child and their family. It enables children to feel safe and cared for, and reassures parents that their child is being responded to sensitively and with care (DCSF, 2008d, 2.4). Some of the challenges of implementing an effective Key Person system are addressed in Chapter 6, and you will be encouraged to explore your role, as an EYP, in developing such an approach and through modelling good practice as a Key Person yourself.

REFLECTIVE TASK

- *What is your experience to date of the Key Person system?*
- *What have you observed as the main benefits to children and families of a KP system?*
- *What do you believe are the benefits to staff and settings?*

Much has been written about the way adults relate to and interact with young children in order to support their learning and development, and the work of Laevers with Heylen (2003) is important in offering us a European perspective on the impact of 'teacher style' on children's learning. The Effective Early Learning (EEL) Project (Pascal and Bertram, 2001) is included in this and identifies three key aspects of the adult's behaviour that have a direct impact on children's learning: levels of sensitivity, the amount of stimulation and the 'allowing' of autonomy. As an EYP, in modelling effective interactions and relationships with children in their play, these are important issues with which to engage and, in Chapter 6, the case studies and practical tasks will support your thinking and reflection on this aspect of your practice.

Sustained shared thinking

One of the newer concepts to be embedded into the EYFS Framework is that of the adult's role in encouraging children's critical and creative thinking skills. Standard 16 requires that the EYP *engages in sustained shared thinking with children* (CWDC, 2008, p34), with further guidance given that this involves *providing planned and seizing un-planned opportunities to improve children's thinking skills by engaging them in high quality verbal interactions*. The phrase was a key feature of the REPEY Report (Siraj-Blatchford *et al.*, 2002a) though it is not actually a *new* concept as such, but – rather – a new term given to the value and potential of adult–child interactions. For instance, Vygotsky's (1978) notions of social interaction and 'more knowledgeable other', Bruner's (1961) concept of 'discovery learning', Lave and Wenger's (1991) 'situated learning' and Bandura's (1977) social learning theory all point to the importance of adult and child sharing learning through sustained shared thinking.

In evidencing this Standard (16), it is important that you are aware of your role in supporting and challenging children's thinking and how you do this. In Chapter 7, there is opportunity to reflect on the following questions (adapted from DCSF, 2008d, 4.3).

- How do I get involved in the thinking process with children?

- How do I develop and maintain my awareness of the children's interests and under-standings, and work together with the children to develop an idea or skill?

- How do I show genuine interest to children, offer them encouragement, clarify what they are thinking and ask open questions?

- What opportunities/resources do I provide for children to discover connections and extend their thinking?

The case studies in Chapter 7 will help you consider what sustained shared thinking might look like, and encourage you to have greater confidence in this area of practice.

Quality indicators

So far, the notion of 'quality' has been largely avoided. This is because it is one that is fraught with challenges in its definition – you might like to think how you would define it. Yet it is also a word that is used commonly to describe 'good' or even 'best' practice and certainly features in much regulatory and advisory documentation. Since 1996, Ofsted has been responsible for registering and inspecting Early Years settings as part of a national programme of *quality regulation.* The past decade has seen the development of a range of different *quality assurance* schemes. The concept of *quality improvement* is now embedded within contemporary Early Years provision and practice (e.g. DCSF, 2008c), and this includes both processes for self-assessment and tools by which practice can be strengthened. EYPS Standard 20 requires you to *be accountable for the delivery of high quality provision* (CWDC, 2008, p80).

What does all this mean in practice? In Chapter 8, we explore further these ideas about and of 'quality' that permeate much of our culture and have impacted directly on Early Years provision and practice. Towards the end of the twentieth century, the Rumbold Report (DES, 1990) on the quality of education for under-fives highlighted the tension that existed then between the *processes* and *outcomes* of learning. It concluded that *how* children learn is as important as *what* children are learning, and the report warned against pressures to overemphasise target-led learning. Ball's (1994) work followed this up and defined 'quality learning' as where children's capacity and motivation to acquire know-ledge, skills and positive attitudes is developed; and where they can make sense of their own world and operate effectively in it. Abbott and Rodger (2003) also picked up on the conclusions of the Rumbold Report, and argued that quality care and education are inseparable. This understanding, sometimes expressed as 'edu-care' (Smith, 1988) is now generally assumed across Early Years practice and provision.

What, then, is the value of quality indicators? Should these be externally defined and prescribed? The work of Sylva *et al.* (2006) and the indicators of quality defined in the Early Childhood Environment Rating Scale (ECERS-E) are discussed as these claim to offer a helpful means for self-assessment and for improving pedagogy in pre-school settings so that young children's learning and development can flourish. This is set alongside Dahlberg *et al.*'s (2006) suggestion that we have now moved *beyond quality,* as it is philosophically impossible to define absolutely and can only be rooted in a specific context that cannot then be translated across boundaries of time and space.

More specifically for you, though, there is opportunity to explore what are commonly held to be 'markers' of good practice. These include meeting individual needs, effective monitoring and tracking of children's progress, good experiences of transitions and continuity within children's learning, and partnerships with families, local communities, other professionals and local authorities. Examples of how EYPs are leading and supporting effective practice are provided to encourage your own reflection on such indicators of high-quality provision.

Continuing professional development

The final chapter in the book summarises the main themes of the previous chapters, and discusses further aspects of the EYP role and accountability. Standards 38 and 39 are the focus here, with a challenge to commit to ongoing continuing professional development by modelling yourself as a 'good learner' to colleagues, children and parents. Siraj-Blatchford and Manni (2007), in their Effective Leadership in Early Years Settings (ELEYS) study, have identified the characteristics or patterns of leadership that can be identified in settings judged to be offering the highest-quality Early Learning experiences for children and families. The study defines one important aspect of the leadership role and support for others to be that of *building a learning community and team culture* (Siraj-Blatchford and Manni, 2007, p21). In demonstrating your own commitment to ongoing learning and development, you are encouraging colleagues to do likewise. The wealth of knowledge, understanding and skills developed and acquired already about Early Years practice and provision is huge, but there is still so much more to learn. It's a truism that the more we know, the more we realise we don't know, and this clearly applies to our knowledge about young children and how they learn and develop.

Global influences on early childhood practices are acknowledged in Chapter 2 but in the final chapter we explore further specific pedagogical models such as the Danish Forest School approach (Knight, 2009), the Reggio Emilia pre-schools in Italy (Edwards *et al.*, 1998), and '*Te Whāriki*', the framework for early childhood in New Zealand (NZME, 1996). Reflective tasks will help you think about how insights from alternative models or approaches do, or might, impact on your own practice and support for others.

We conclude the book by discussing EYP Networks, and their role in establishing and promoting a distinctive sense of professional identity. The new model or paradigm that befits Early Years Professional Status is, in part, being informed and shaped by you – the EYPs yourselves – and we explore some of ways the EYP role is developing. While EYPs represent a wide range of backgrounds, qualifications and experience, common ground is found when each of you takes the opportunity to reflect on your own strengths, and to identify appropriate and often innovative ways of supporting the effective practice of others.

REFLECTIVE TASK

- *To what extent do you see yourself as a 'reflective practitioner'?*

- *How do you model this to colleagues?*

C H A P T E R   S U M M A R Y

This books aims to support you as you prepare for the EYP validation process. In particular, it focuses on your role as an effective practitioner and in supporting the effective practice of others. The case studies of other EYPs, or those aspiring to the role, that you will encounter in this book are here to help you reflect on your own role. The more you are aware of *what* you do, *why* you do it that way and the *impact* of this on children, the more you are reflecting on your practice, developing and learning and acting as that vital 'agent of change'. In this way, you will be *developing [your] pedagogy* (DCSF, 2009a, p4).

Moving on

The contents of the book have been outlined and – it is hoped – this has whetted your appetite for reflection on what it means to support effective practice within the EYP role. In the next chapter, the focus is primarily on relevant research projects and other studies on concepts of 'quality' and 'effectiveness' in Early Years practice. Standards 1–6 require evidence of knowledge and understanding of principles, policy and practice. The EYP who is genuinely committed to the highest-quality delivery will keep abreast of key research findings in order to consolidate, update and enhance his/her own knowledge and understanding.

Self-assessment task

As you begin to explore your understanding of what constitutes effective practice, think about the dimensions of the EYP role offered in Whalley *et al.*'s (2008) definition. Are you able to begin to identify examples from your own practice and link these to the EYP Standards?

The EYP role	Example from practice	Links to EYP Standards
Reflective and reflexive practice		
Skills in decision making		
Sound knowledge and understanding of Early Years pedagogy		
Strong values of the intrinsic worth of each child and all those in their world		
The ability to role model, lead and support others in high-quality practice		
The ability to define a vision for practice within a setting		
Competence as an agent of change		

FURTHER READING

Allen, SF and Wilson, D (2008) Meeting the challenges of leading practice, in Whalley, ME, Allen, SF and Wilson, D (eds) *Leading Practice in Early Years Settings.* Exeter: Learning Matters.

Siraj-Blatchford, I, Sylva, K, Muttock, S, Gilden, R and Bell, D (2002) *Researching Effective Pedagogy in the Early Years.* Research Brief (RB 356). London: DfES.

2   Perspectives on Early Years pedagogy

CHAPTER OBJECTIVES

Early Years Professionals (EYPs) are required to demonstrate at graduate level sound knowledge and understanding of the pedagogical principles that underpin effective practice. This chapter explores the influence of the early pioneers and reformers, some of the classic theories of early learning and development, and contemporary key research studies that inform such pedagogical principles. However, none of these is simply addressed 'academically' but, through practical and reflective tasks and case studies, there is opportunity to see how, in turn, research has shaped current Early Years practice in general and understanding of the EYP role in particular.

After reading this chapter you should be able to:
* discuss contemporary understanding of Early Years pedagogy;
* reflect on a range of research studies and how these have contributed to greater understanding of effective practice;
* apply some of these insights from theory and research to your own practice as you begin to articulate your own pedagogy.

This chapter offers links to many of the EYP Standards and, in particular, to Standards 1, 2, 38 and 39.

Introduction

That word 'pedagogy'

The term 'pedagogy' still does not enjoy widespread currency in the United Kingdom, despite being commonly used elsewhere in Europe and, indeed, in many other parts of the world. As we have noted, pedagogy has a general meaning of the art or science of teaching. It is important not to confuse 'pedagogy' with 'curriculum' or simply 'teaching', but to think of it as *any conscious action by one person designed to enhance learning in another* (Mortimore, 1999, p3) or any *activity that promotes learning* (Stephen, 2006). Within Early Years, a distinctive understanding of pedagogy has been emerging over the past few decades, informed by both classic learning and developmental theory, and a number of more recent research studies and projects. It is this broader and more distinctive understanding that we consider here. The concept of Early Years pedagogy may be unfamiliar to you but the strength and effectiveness of your practice does need to be supported by what might be called a sound 'pedagogical base'.

Theoretical influences

Pedagogy can also be viewed as a *body of theory and practice that draws on philosophy, psychology and social science* (Cameron, 2006, p9). As an EYP, you are required to demonstrate knowledge and understanding of the *principles and content of the EYFS* and *the individual and diverse ways in which [young] children develop* (Standards 1 and 2, CWDC, 2008, pp14–15), which draw essentially on theoretical insights from philosophy, psychology and social science. Other books in this series (Ingleby and Oliver, 2008; Palaiologou, 2008) cover some of these in much more detail than space allows here and, indeed, there are any number of reputable academic sources of information to provide you with essential background reading on these matters; one in particular is signposted in the 'Further reading' section at the end of this chapter. In seeking to understand the concept and practice of pedagogy, however, it would be a huge omission not to acknowledge the debt owed to those Early Years pioneers, reformers and theorists who have exercised such influence on the pedagogical basis for practice as we know it today.

Ideas and thinking about how children learn and develop have evolved over the past 300 years and more. Such thinking has informed and shaped a range of approaches to Early Years 'curricula' (not a word favoured by the authors in an Early Years context but used, loosely, to describe 'established frameworks for learning and development') and understanding of the role of the Early Years practitioner. Many of you will have covered aspects of this 'thinking' in previous studies but it is always useful to revise and review our understandings.

A timeline of theorists and pioneers who have had particular influence in the development of Western Early Years pedagogy and practice would probably start with the French philosopher, Rousseau (1712–78), who stressed that young children should be allowed to develop free of society's constraints, and that provision for them should provide a balance between *freedom and happiness on the one hand and increasing independence and control on the other* (Roopnarine and Johnson, 1987, cited in Johnston and Nahmad-Williams, 2009). Such a timeline would continue through Pestalozzi (1746–1827), the Swiss educational reformer, whose influence on primary education has been huge, and encompass Froebel (1782–1852), a German educator, who introduced the concept of the kindergarten, the American John Dewey (1859–1952), who is generally held to be responsible for the gradual shift from school-centred towards a more child-centred pedagogy – especially in the Early Years (Browne, 2007) – and Montessori (1870–1952), an Italian educator and doctor, who introduced the Montessori Method based on child-centred, though *not* child-led, principles (Montessori, 1912). The Montessori Method remains in evidence in settings across the world.

In the UK, the McMillan sisters, Rachel (1859–1917) and Margaret (1860–1931), were committed to the social welfare of children and the reform necessary to achieve this for all. They opened England's first nursery schools, recognising that children learn most effectively when they are well fed and clothed, and the learning environment is organised to protect their health and welfare (McMillan, 1930). Steiner (1861–1925), an Austrian philosopher and scientist, developed the philosophical doctrine of anthroposophy, emphasising the spiritual growth of human beings through the educational processes of 'doing', 'thinking' and 'feeling' (Oldfield, 2001). Steiner schools are gaining wider recognition in England. Susan Isaacs (1885–1948), from Bolton, England, also exerted significant influence upon our understanding of Early Years practice. Her lasting contribution has been on the importance of play and the value of child observations (Willan, 2009).

PRACTICAL TASK

From the summary above, take any one of these early pioneers/reformers and investigate in more detail her/his philosophy and beliefs. Then reflect on how this pioneer has informed the Four Themes in the EYFS Framework (DCSF, 2008e), listed in the table below. You may choose to do this for more than one.

The Unique Child
Positive Relationships
Enabling Environments
Learning and Development

Source: adapted from Palaiologou (2008, p21)

It may be helpful to discuss your evaluation with a colleague.

Developmental approaches to children's learning

As we see from the EYFS themes (DCSF, 2008e), 'learning' and 'development' are inseparable in Early Years pedagogy. Studies of early childhood focus on the different aspects of learning and development: physical, cognitive/intellectual, linguistic, social and emotional. More recently, 'cultural' and 'spiritual' development have joined these. You may be familiar with such 'compartmentalisation' from your earlier study? Arguably, this way of viewing learning and development is both helpful and unhelpful. An understanding of some of the classic theories of child development and learning offers a rationale for such compartmentalisation and allows practitioners to address all areas of learning and development from an informed perspective. However, in any such consideration, it should be remembered that, essentially, Early Years pedagogy assumes a much more holistic stance – seeing the child as a whole, with a body, mind, emotions, creativity and social identity (Moss and Petrie, 2002).

Standard 2 focuses clearly on the EYP's knowledge and understanding of child develop-ment, and we turn now to a number of developmental psychologists whose influence on practice has been seminal. No reference to this discipline would be complete without reference to Piaget, the Swiss developmental biologist whose stage theory of development (Piaget, 1952; Piaget and Inhelder, 1969) has had a hugely powerful influence on educational thinking and curriculum development. (see Appendix 1). Although challenged by later writers (e.g. Donaldson, 1978; James *et al.*, 1998), with accumulated evidence suggesting that this model is much too rigid and a number of his original observations flawed, Piaget's theory has undoubtedly had a major influence on the way Early Years settings organise provision, with children grouped by age/developmental stage. Possibly, his most enduring influence has been on our understanding that children learn actively through exploration within a stimulating environment (Stephen, 2006). Piaget's concepts of schemas, assimilation, accommodation and equilibration have also had significant influ-ence on our understanding of how young children learn and develop (see Appendix 2).

A number of other theorists have also contributed to our understanding of Early Years pedagogy and practice. Vygotsky (1896–1934), a Russian teacher and psychologist, took a different view to the behaviourist and Piagetian (constructivist) approach, and is better known as a *socio*-constructivist because of his emphasis on the social world of the child.

Identifying the importance of cultural tools for making meaning, Vygotsky emphasised the particular significance of language in children's development, and that learning occurs most effectively through interaction and talk with skilled adults, and through social interaction with peers (Vygotsky and Cole, 1978). Vygotsky's identification of the 'zone of the proximal development (ZPD)' – *which is the difference between tested levels of cognitive development and potential development that can be achieved through interaction with adults* (Johnston and Nahmad-Williams, 2009, p28) – has been parti-cularly influential in informing and evaluating pedagogical approaches in early childhood settings.

Rogoff (1990), who promotes a socio-cultural understanding of learning, extended Vygotsky's ZPD, proposing the concept of 'guided participation' as a more inclusive framework for analysing how young children learn through active participation in everyday social activities with an adult or more experienced peer to master tasks just beyond their reach. Both Vygotsky's ZPD and Rogoff's notion of 'guided participation' are particularly pertinent for the EYP and many of the Standards, especially those classified as 'Effective Practice' and 'Relationships with Children' (Standards 7–24, CWDC, 2008, pp21, 45), provide opportunities for you to demonstrate skills in interacting with young children and recognising their active participation in the learning environment.

Vygotsky also carried out detailed analysis of children's play and concluded, as Isaacs had, that play was as significant for social/emotional development as for cognitive and physical development.

The behaviourist theory of development has its roots in the work of John Locke (1632–1704), and includes the work of Watson, Pavlov and Skinner. Based on well-known experiments, such as Pavlov's salivating dogs (Pavlov, 1927) and Skinner's rats (Slater, 2004), the principles of behaviourism developed thus:

- children learn through reinforcement or punishment; thus learning is acquired rather than innate;

- stimuli for learning in the environment are critical.

For the behaviourist, then, learning is *changes in behaviour which occur as the result of experience and interactions with the environment* (Glassman, 2000) and includes the concepts of rewards and sanctions, and positive and negative reinforcement. Behaviourist theory was challenged and developed by Bandura (1977), a Canadian developmental psychologist, who argued that the idea that it is the environment that causes behaviour is too simplistic, and it is social and cultural environments that are critical to human development. His social learning theory, based largely on his famous Bobo Doll experiments (Bandura, 1973) suggests that children are continuously learning through observation and imitation of significant others – parents, carers/educators and peers.

Bowlby's (1958, 1960a, 1960b) theory of attachment remains highly controversial, but has contributed to our understanding of young children's need for secure bonds with the adults who care for them. Bowlby, with his medical background, carried out observations that led him to identify the early attachment that occurs between a baby and the primary carer (usually the mother), and to conclude that a child's experience of this was vital to subsequent development. Bowlby's work was extended, refined – even challenged – by Schaffer and Emerson (1964), Ainsworth and Bell (1970), and others. Bowlby's theory has given rise to ongoing debate about care in the home versus care in an Early Years setting, which is clearly *continually pertinent* (Johnston and Nahmad-Williams, 2009). Yet, the importance placed on the Key Person system (Elfer *et al.*, 2003) – especially at times of transition – one of the statutory requirements of the EYFS (DCSF, 2008a), demonstrates how far reaching attachment theory is.

There are many other theorists we might mention, but a further three are particularly worthy of brief inclusion here. Bruner has contributed significantly to our understanding of cognitive development. Of particular pertinence to Early Years pedagogy and practice, he identified three modes of representation that enable the individual to make sense or meaning of their world (Bruner, 1966). Based on Piaget's (1952) theory, Bruner similarly describes three stages – though less rigidly linked to chronological age – which he calls the enactive, iconic and then symbolic levels of cognitive development. At the enactive stage, the child manipulates materials directly; at the iconic level, s/he can deal with mental images of objects and does not need to manipulate them directly; finally, the child moves to the symbolic level where s/he no longer needs either objects or mental images but can conceptualise symbolically and deal with abstract and flexible thoughts. Bruner also developed Vygotsky's earlier work on the ZPD and introduced the concept of 'scaffolding' (Bruner, 1978), based on the belief that, for effective learning to take place, the adult must provide a framework that is always one step ahead of the child.

Gardner's (1993) theory of multiple intelligences signified a 'paradigm shift' (Smith and Smith, 1994) from the idea that intelligence is a single entity, measured by testing, to a much broader understanding of a *set* of intelligences. Although Gardner described these as seven (later nine) separate dimensions of intelligence (Gardner, 1993, 1999), he argues that they will rarely operate independently but, rather, combine to complement each other as individuals develop a range of skills and learn how to address challenges and solve problems. The original list of seven intelligences is as follows (adapted from Smith, 2008).

1. Linguistic intelligence: sensitivity to spoken and written language; the ability to learn and use language.

2. Logical-mathematical intelligence: the capacity to analyse problems logically, mathematically and scientifically.

3. Musical intelligence: skills in performance, composition and musical aurality.

4. Bodily: kinaesthetic intelligence – the athletic potential of using the whole or parts of the body to solve problems.

5. Spatial intelligence: the potential to recognise and use the patterns and shape of space, small and large.

6. Interpersonal intelligence: the capacity to understand the intentions, motivations and desires of other people and to work effectively with them.

7. Intrapersonal intelligence: the capacity to understand oneself and one's feelings in order to have effective self-awareness.

Such thinking has been highly influential, particularly in the USA, and has been embraced particularly among educational theorists and teachers, from pre-school to higher education. Arguably, Gardner's lasting contribution is in helping us have a broader vision of learning and education and that, rather than overemphasising the first two (which have been the traditional focus of teaching and learning), all intelligences are needed to live life well. Within the EYFS, the six areas of learning (DSCF, 2008a) are now all seen as equally important in providing broad and balanced opportunities for early learning.

Bronfenbrenner is our final theorist here. His ecological systems theory (Bronfenbrenner, 1979) views the child as developing within a complex system of relationships – each affected by the other. The four systems, which he conceptualises as a 'nested structure' (much like the Russian dolls of his birth country), are as follows.

1. The microsystem: that closest to the child and that involves the child's immediate surroundings refers to the primary relationships within the family and neighbourhood.

2. The mesosystem: this is 'once removed' from the actual child (the home, Early Years setting, school, place of worship, the community in which the child lives and plays), and involves key interactions and relationships between those connected to the child's microsystems (e.g. children's relationships with other children, parents, teachers).

3. The exosystem: the wider social system, including housing, employment and the economic climate – here the child is not actually directly involved at all, but the exosystem includes important structures and networks that provide wider support, such as parents' workplaces, places of worship and community links.

4. The macrosystem: the system furthest removed from the actual child – involving the cultural values, legal infrastructure and wider socio-economic context in which the child is developing.

Bronfenbrenner's holistic approach to childcare highlights that children's participation in different environments impacts on their experience of each one. Such a theory suggests, for instance, that understandings of childhood and the value placed on it inform and influence government policy on investment in childhood services (the macrosystem), which then directly impacts on the child's world (the microsystem). Conversely, understanding of childhood is itself derived from the children of a particular community – based on professional observation of their needs and experiences. This, of course, will differ from community to community.

PRACTICAL TASK

A number of complex theories have been outlined very briefly here. You now have further opportunity to think about the link between some of these key theories and your own work and practice as an EYP in leading delivery of the EYFS.

All the theories outlined link directly to Standard 2 and, less directly, to Standard 1. Look at some of the other EYP Standards (listed in the table below) and see if you can identify a major theory, theorist and/or reformer/pioneer whose work has informed each.

Standard	Links to theorist/theory and/or pioneer/reformer
03 How children's well-being, development, learning and behaviour can be affected by a range of influences and transitions from inside and outside the setting . . .	
05 The current legal requirements, national policies on health and safety, safeguarding and promoting the well-being of children . . .	
10 Use close, informed observation and other strategies to monitor children's activity, development and progress systematically and carefully . . .	
17 Promote positive behaviour, self-control and independence through using effective behaviour management strategies and developing children's social, emotional and behavioural skills . . .	
23 Identify and support children whose progress, development or well-being is affected by changes or difficulties in their personal circumstances . . .	

Standard	Links to theorist/theory and/or pioneer/reformer
27 Listen to children, pay attention to what they say and value and respect their views . . .	
28 Demonstrate the positive values, attitudes and behaviour they expect from children . . .	
29 Recognise and respect the influential and enduring contribution that families and parents/carers can make to children's development, well-being and learning . . .	

Learning from contemporary research

In the previous sections, we saw the breadth of global influence on Early Years pedagogy and practice. Here we consider some recent research studies from England. You are encouraged to read these more fully for yourself (most can be downloaded freely). These have been selected here because they are judged to have informed and shaped both the EYFS Framework (DCSF, 2008a) and the EYP Standards and, when the main findings from each have been outlined – and you have been able to read further for yourselves – you will have opportunity to reflect on their significance for the contemporary Children's Workforce and, specifically, on your own role and practice. This will give you the chance to think of the wider context of your practice and be open to deepening your own understanding. Remember, Standards 38 and 39 provide you with opportunity to reflect creatively on practice issues. This can result in a shift in thinking as well as in changes to practice.

The Effective Provision of Pre-school Education (EPPE) project (Sylva *et al.*, 2003)

The EPPE project is a large-scale, mixed-method, longitudinal study tracking the progress and development of around 3,000 children (aged from three years) over an extended period. The first phase of the project (Sylva *et al.*, 2003) investigated the effects of pre-school provision (or none) on the children, aiming to identify the impact of a range of child, parent, home and pre-school influences on children's attainment and social behaviour. Key findings show that pre-school experience (compared to none) enhances children's development and that an earlier start at settings relates to better outcomes for children in terms of cognitive development, improved independence, concentration and sociability. Disadvantaged children particularly benefit from good quality pre-school experiences though, interestingly, it was found that full-time attendance leads to no greater benefits than part-time for any child.

The Researching Effective Pedagogy in the Early Years (REPEY) project (Siraj-Blatchford *et al.*, 2002a)

The EPPE project (Sylva *et al.*, 2003) did not set out directly to contribute to our understanding of effective pedagogy but from the EPPE data a small number of case studies were identified to provide more detailed, qualitative understanding of the characteristics of effective practice and the pedagogical understanding that underpins these. This evolved into the Researching Effective Pedagogy in the Early Years (REPEY) project (Siraj-Blatchford *et al.*, 2002a) where the authors aimed to identify the pedagogical strategies and techniques that affect child outcomes. In particular, the outcomes of REPEY relate specifically to conceptualising the relationship between play-based pedagogy and high-quality provision. In summary, the findings show that the most effective settings are those that view cognitive and social development as complementary, and the key finding defined effective pedagogy as *both the kind of interaction traditionally associated with the term 'teaching' and the provision of instructive learning and play environments and routines* (Siraj-Blatchford *et al.*, 2002b, p1). The REPEY findings have significant relevance to our discussion of sustained shared thinking in Chapter 7.

The Study of Pedagogical Effectiveness in Early Learning (SPEEL) project (Moyles *et al.*, 2002a)

While the REPEY project (Siraj-Blatchford *et al.*, 2002a) concentrated on child factors that inform pedagogy, the authors of the SPEEL project (Moyles *et al.*, 2002a) increasingly focused their research on identifiable components of pedagogy and the adult role. The main outcome of the research was the Framework for Effective Pedagogy in the Early Years, which Moyles *et al.* (2002b, p1) describe as a *set of quality assurance criteria* and *aspirational . . . in identifying the highest level of effectiveness*. The Framework comprises 129 key statements classified under three main areas of focus: Practice, Principles and Professional Dimensions. Although the Framework has not been adopted in its entirety, it nevertheless offers a useful checklist of skills, knowledge and attributes that are requisite of the effective Early Years practitioner, and was the first research study of its kind to isolate and record the effects of adult pedagogy on children's learning.

REFLECTIVE TASK

Read through the 129 Key Statements on the Framework for Effective Pedagogy in the Early Years (Moyles et al., 2002a). (You will find this at: www.dcsf.gov.uk/research/data/uploadfiles/RR363.pdf, Section 4, from pages 48–58.) Reflect on how these identify the characteristics of professionalism that are embedded in the EYP Standards.

The Early Years Transition and Special Educational Needs (EYTSEN) project (Sammons *et al.*, 2003)

The EYTSEN study also builds on the longitudinal EPPE project to *explore the relationship between the quality of pre-school settings, their pedagogy and child, family and home environment characteristics which contribute to effective cognitive and social/behavioural development in children* (Sammons *et al.*, 2003, p2). While recognising that the term 'special educational needs' (SEN) is not always appropriately applied to very young children, nonetheless this study sought to identify children who might be 'at risk' of developing SEN in either cognitive development, behavioural development or both. In particular, the researchers sought to examine the impact of pre-school provision on such 'at risk' children, to consider the existing practices in identifying and supporting them and to *illuminate the factors . . . that might 'protect' children from developing SEN* (Sammons *et al.*, 2003, p3). Findings showed that the number of children presenting as *at [cognitive] risk* as they started pre-school fell from a third to a fifth on entry to school, suggesting the positive impact of effective pre-school provision on cognitive development. This was particularly marked for those children considered to be most disadvantaged and vulnerable. However, the systems in place for identifying and addressing children with SEN were variable so some 'at risk' children were missing the opportunity for early intervention.

PRACTICAL TASK

In the table below you will find some of the key findings from the four research studies outlined above. Using your copy of Guidance to the Standards for the Award of Early Years Professional Status *(CWDC, 2008) complete the table to show (a) influence on EYFS practice and (b) links to the EYP Standards.*

Study	Key finding	Impact on contemporary EYFS practice	Links to EYP Standards
EPPE (Sylva *et al.*, 2003)	The duration of attendance at a pre-school setting is important, with an earlier start being related to better cognitive development, and improved independence, concentration and sociability		
	Where settings view educational and social development as complementary and equal in importance, children make better all-round progress		
	Settings that have staff with higher qualifications . . . generally provide higher-quality provision and children make more progress		

Study	Key finding	Impact on contemporary EYFS practice	Links to EYP Standards
REPEY (Siraj-Blatchford *et al.*, 2002a)	Adult–child interactions that involve 'sustained shared thinking' and open-ended questioning extend children's learning		
	There are good outcomes for children when practitioners have good knowledge of early learning and understanding of child development		
	There are good outcomes for children when educational aims and programmes are shared with parents		
	Good outcomes for children are linked to formative feedback during activities		
SPEEL (Moyles *et al.*, 2002a)	The vastness and complexity of what constitutes effective pedagogy came as a surprise to most of the practitioners in the study		
	Effective pedagogical practices are dependent on all practitioners feeling that they are important, valued and have status		
	The most effective practitioners are those who are conscious of their impact on children's learning		
EYTSEN (Sammons *et al.*, 2003)	Understandings of what constitutes SEN varies across settings, and poor cognitive development may not always be recognised as a 'need' in pre-school		

PRACTICAL TASK *continued*

Study	Key finding	Impact on contemporary EYFS practice	Links to EYP Standards
	The majority of parents were satisfied with the support their children were given for SEN but, where they were dissatisfied, they wanted more learning on an individual basis		
	High-quality pre-school provision can be seen as an effective intervention that can help improve cognitive development and provide children with a better start		

The social pedagogue

When the draft proposals for the new professional status in the developing children's workforce were circulated (CWDC, 2005), one of the suggested titles for the role was that of the 'social pedagogue'. This drew specifically on the Danish model of Early Years graduate professionals. Across Denmark, it is social pedagogues who are the main workers in nurseries and other children's settings. Other continental European countries operate a similar system, with a shared understanding of the role, though in some the role is known simply as the 'pedagogue'. While, for a wide range of reasons, following consultation on the draft proposals, this term was rejected in favour of the 'Early Years Professional', brief appraisal of the concept of the social pedagogue can support our understanding of the pedagogical base for the EYP role in leading effective practice.

The concept of the 'social pedagogue', first defined in nineteenth-century Germany (Petrie *et al.*, 2005), has its roots in an understanding that pedagogy goes way beyond learning associated with traditional schooling and, as a concept, is founded on humanistic values and an image of children as active agents and competent, resourceful human beings. Kornbeck (2002) describes social pedagogy as the provision of social welfare, all that makes for well-being, based on pedagogic principles. Such a model fits easily in an Early Years context where children are seen as developing in different ways and at different rates, and the adult role as one of *supporting children's learning within an enabling, facilitating and observing role rather than directly as 'teachers'* (Moyles *et al.*, 2002a). The social pedagogue emphasises the relationship with the child as a whole being, supporting all aspects of development equally and working with each child to establish positive dispositions for learning. Can you see the parallels here with the vision for the EYP role as *key to raising the quality of Early Years provision and exercising leadership in making a positive difference to children's well-being, learning and development* (CWDC, 2008, p5)?

Self-assessment task

In pedagogy, care and education meet.

(Petrie *et al.*, 2005, p2)

Look at Standard 7 and reflect on opportunities you have in your current setting to demonstrate effective pedagogy. Think about the following questions.

- How do you demonstrate your high expectations while also focusing on the child as a 'whole being'?

- In what ways are care and education inseparably rooted in your understanding of effective pedagogy?

- What specific examples of the above can you identify within your own practice and/or leadership of others?

Child-centredness and play

Among Early Years practitioners, there would be little dispute about what constitutes the core of effective practice: *child-centredness* and *play*. Indeed, guidance from DCSF (2009a) is an indicator of how significant play is in 'good' Early Years practice. However, there is less universal agreement on what these two concepts actually mean (Chung and Walsh, 2000; Siraj-Blatchford and Sylva, 2004). Were you aware that there has been very little direct reference in any of the above reports to these two 'core concepts' of Early Years pedagogy? Stephen (2010, p3) refers to these as the two 'Big Ideas' about Early Years pedagogy; yet, she also highlights that both terms are very difficult to define. In a review of early childhood literature, Chung and Walsh (2000) found the term 'child-centredness' to have at least 40 different meanings, ranging from concerns with children's interests to their participation in decision making. Siraj-Blatchford and Sylva's 2004 study, in fact, highlighted that it is a balance between child-*initiated* and practitioner-*initiated* activities that are most effective, with less emphasis on activities that are 'led'.

Our understanding of play has developed from some of the pioneers and reformers, such as Vygotsky and Isaacs. The role of the EYP in providing effective play opportunities is addressed in more detail in the next chapter and also in Chapter 6, but it is worth noting here that defining a play-based pedagogy is problematic. The British Educational Research Association (BERA) Early Years Special Interest Group (2003, p14) identified that *while play forms the bedrock of early learning, an agreed pedagogy of play is less well-articulated . . . and not underpinned by systematic empirical research . . . [with] significant gaps between the rhetoric and reality of play*. As an EYP, it is important that you engage with such debate and look critically at what you understand by 'play'. As Stephen (2010, p4) notes, one purpose of reviewing the place of play in early learning is to strengthen its place *as a medium for learning when that is most appropriate, to ensure that the play opportunities offered to children are playful and engaging to them and to develop a more . . . evidence-based rationale for play*. Look at how one EYP has changed her understanding of the place of play in early learning.

Alexandria

Alexandria is a practitioner with over 20 years' experience in a range of Early Years settings: private, voluntary and maintained. She has worked in her current workplace for six years and is now the room leader in the pre-school department (three to four year olds) of a large private nursery. This involves leading the team of five other practitioners in EYFS delivery. Alexandria is currently on the long pathway to EYPS, having completed a Foundation Degree, and is now studying for an honours degree. Alexandria describes her own learning journey as follows.

Since my early training, I had always just 'known' that play was important for children but know now that I had a tendency to just 'let them play' as they wished, so long as this was round the routine of the day – snack, lunchtime, story time etc. More recently, especially as I've been reading about play and reflecting on my own practice, I've been able to think much more about my role in children's play and what quality play really means. I encouraged each of the other staff to observe their key children at play and identify how they might extend children's learning in this by getting actively involved, almost turn-taking . . . following the children's ideas and then making some suggestions of our own. This has worked very well in imaginative play situations and we believe we've seen some examples of really deep learning. I've had my ideas about what play is turned on their head – and now know that the important thing is that children are deeply involved but appropriately supported in their play.

- *What does Alexandria's statement here tell you about her understanding of effective pedagogy and the place of play in this?*

- *In what ways is she gathering an 'evidence-based rationale for play'?*

- *How is your reading of recent research studies combining with your own 'evidence base' to support your own understanding of Early Years pedagogy?*

New and emerging theories

Much of the research cited so far concentrates on children from three years and up and, although space is limited, it is appropriate to focus here briefly on children under two. There is now a growing bank of knowledge linked to neuro-science and neuro-physiology, which has identified processes of brain development and the transmission, storage and retrieval of information (knowledge and understanding) in the memory. Synaptic formation (synaptogenesis) and connections occur at a rapid rate in the first two years of life. Some such synaptic connections, however, are wiped out or 'pruned' (Bee and Boyd,

2007) but evidence is emerging that, each time an experience stimulates a neural pathway, the 'signal' left behind is strengthened and the pathway gradually becomes immune to pruning. Implications for practice are just beginning to emerge and the critical importance of providing a stimulating environment (addressed further in Chapter 5) for these younger children is now permeating more widely.

Another research study that focused on very early development is the Family, Children and Child Care (FCCC) Project (Sylva *et al.*, 2005), which set out to examine the short- and longer-term effects of childcare – in a variety of settings – on children's development between birth and school entry. Research outcomes considered include: health, growth, social and emotional development, and cognitive and educational development. The results are published online in a series of short reports covering different outcomes of the study. One set of results in particular shows that, among children of 18 months, those experiencing quality centre-based care for 12 hours or more a week are predicted higher cognitive development and levels of self-regulation (Sylva *et al.*, 2005). As an EYP, it is important that you demonstrate your knowledge and understanding of, and commitment to, effective practice with children from birth.

C H A P T E R   S U M M A R Y

We have considered here major studies that draw on data from the English context, and also seen the wider global context – albeit primarily the Western world – in which Early Years pedagogy and practice has evolved and is continuing to do so. European influence on the development of the EYP role in the paradigm of the Danish 'social pedagogue' has been outlined. Increasingly, socio-cultural factors are seen to shape our understanding of pedagogy and, indeed, many subscribe to the view that *pedagogy is about learning, teaching and development, influenced by the cultural, social and political values and principles [held] for children [in a particular country] and underpinned by a strong theoretical and practical base* (Learning and Teaching Scotland, 2005, p9). This fits very clearly with the holistic view of the child at the heart of Early Years pedagogy (Moss and Petrie, 2002).

Historically, there has been little evidence of practitioners', including EYPs', willingness to articulate a clear pedagogical basis for their practice (Moyles *et al.*, 2002a; Stephen, 2010) or to think of themselves as pedagogues (Jackson, 2005). However, there are indications that this may be changing (Osgood, 2006; McGillivray, 2008) and with an increasing sense of professionalism permeating the Early Years workforce – not least through the establishment of the EYP role – you have a clear window of opportunity to *create a model of [Early Years] workforce that belongs to the workforce itself, with constructs of professional identity informed by a shared vision and understanding* (McGillivray, 2008, p252). As an EYP, in developing a deeper understanding of the meaning of pedagogy and embedding it into your thinking, language and practice, you will be making your contribution towards a more equal dialogue with the global Early Years community and be in a position to 'engage more fully in international debate and discussion' (Learning and Teaching Scotland, 2005, p8).

Moving on

In the next chapter, there are further opportunities to engage with issues of young children's learning and development. The focus here is on the role of the EYP in developing a play-based approach to leading practice within the EYFS, and you will have further opportunity to reflect on your own knowledge, skills and understanding of the EYP Standards that relate to supporting effective practice.

FURTHER
READING

Johnston, J and Nahmad-Williams, L (2009) *Early Childhood Studies.* London: Pearson/Longman: Chapter 1: 'Theories and theorists'.

McGillivray, G (2008) Nannies, nursery nurses and Early Years professionals: constructions of professional identity in the Early Years workforce in England. *European Early Childhood Research Journal*, 16(2): 242–254.

3 Children's learning and development

CHAPTER OBJECTIVES

This chapter explores the area of young children's learning and development within the context of the Early Years Foundation Stage (EYFS) framework, which sets the standards for the learning, development and care that children should experience in Early Years settings. The provision of play opportunities that are intended to support and extend young children's learning and development is discussed and reflective tasks are included that link to relevant EYP Standards that are mostly, though not entirely, located in the group of standards, 'Knowledge and Understanding' and 'Effective Practice' (CWDC, 2008).

After reading this chapter you should be able to:
- reflect on aspects of Early Years practice that support the learning and development of children from birth to five years across the Early Years Foundation Stage (EYFS);
- consider a play-based approach to children's learning, which is embedded within the EYFS;
- begin to apply your knowledge and understanding of the EYP Standards to your own experience of supporting and extending young children's learning and development.

Introduction

Since September 2008, all children have *been entitled to access a single, evidence-driven, play-based early learning framework – the Early Years Foundation Stage (EYFS)* (DCSF, 2008g, p47). Early Years Professionals (EYPs) work with others to support young children's learning and development within the context of the guidance and statutory requirements that are set out in the EYFS. The Statutory Framework states that Early Years provision must comply with *the learning and development requirements, and the welfare requirements* (DCSF, 2008a, p8) and that *ongoing assessment is an integral part of the learning and development process* (DCSF, 2008a, p16). This chapter, therefore, begins with an outline of the four guiding themes of the EYFS – *A Unique Child, Positive Relationships, Enabling Environments* and *Learning and Development* – which are intended to work together within the delivery of the EYFS across provision for children from birth to five years of age (DCSF, 2008d).

The EYFS: themes, principles and commitments

Each of the four guiding themes has a corresponding principle, which, in turn, has four supporting commitments that explain how the principles can be implemented in practice. The four themes, their linked principles and respective commitments are clearly represented on the poster that is available in the EYFS Pack and, as an attachment, on the EYFS Resources section of the National Strategies website (see www.nationalstrategies. standards.dcsf.gov.uk/eyfs/site/principles/index.htm).

This resource can be a useful aid for your communication about the interconnected nature of the guiding themes of the EYFS and its principled approach to practice when working with practitioners and parents alike. The themes and linked principles all refer to key underpinning aspects of practice that support children's learning and development. The Principles into Practice (PiP) cards (DCSF, 2008e) are another important EYFS resource that expand the core message of each commitment, and support practitioners to implement the EYFS principles. An overview of the EYFS themes and principles, with expanded detail of each commitment is provided in Table 3.1.

Table 3.1 shows how the EYFS places the child as an active learner, competent from birth and able to learn by following their interests and through interactions with others. The EYFS emphasises practitioners' crucial role in extending and developing children's language and communication in their play (DCSF, 2008d). This perception draws on the work of Vygotsky (1978), a key proponent of the social and cultural approach to learning (see Chapter 2). Vygotsky emphasised how 'verbal communication with adults becomes a powerful factor in the development of the child's concepts' (Vygotsky, 1986, p123). This view is acknowledged in S16, which is concerned with the EYP's role to develop children's thinking skills, *by engaging them in high quality verbal interactions involving sustained, shared thinking* (CWDC, 2008, p34). We explore this further in Chapter 6.

Play and exploration

The EYFS has a clear message about the place of play in children's learning. The PiP Card 4.1, for instance, states that *in their play, children learn at their highest level* (DCSF, 2008e). This view is supported by Moyles (2010, p27), who, reflecting on recent research into play (see, e.g., Broadhead, 2008; Tovey, 2008), asserts that play is *the most powerful medium for learning in the early years*.

Despite the importance attached to play within the EYFS, 'play' cannot be so readily categorised or defined (Wood and Attfield, 2005). The following list, however, helps us to consider *behaviours and actions of play* (Moyles, 2010, p24).

- Play is intrinsically motivated.

- The play process is more important than the outcome it produces.

- Everything is possible – reality can be disregarded and imagination allowed to take over.

Table 3.1 Overview of EYFS Themes, Principles and Commitments

Theme 1: A Unique Child	Theme 2: Positive Relationships	Theme 3: Enabling Environments	Theme 4: Learning and Development
Linked Principle: Every child is a competent learner from birth who can be resilient, capable, confident and self-assured.	**Linked Principle:** Children learn to be strong and independent from a base of loving and secure relationships with parents and/or a Key Person.	**Linked Principle:** The environment plays a key role in supporting and extending children's development and learning.	**Linked Principle:** Children develop and learn in different ways and at different rates, and all areas of Learning and Development are equally important and interconnected.
Supporting Commitments: *1.1 Child Development* Babies and children develop in individual ways and at varying rates. Every area of development – physical, cognitive, linguistic, spiritual, social and emotional – is equally important.	**Supporting Commitments:** *2.1 Respecting Each Other* Every interaction is based on caring professional relationships and respectful acknowledgement of the feelings of children and their families.	**Supporting Commitments:** *3.1 Observation, Assessment and Planning* Babies and young children are individuals first, each with a unique profile of abilities. Schedules and routines should flow with the child's needs. All planning starts with observing children in order to understand and consider their current interests, development and learning.	**Supporting Commitments:** *4.1 Play and Exploration* Children's play reflects their wide-ranging and varied interests and preoccupations. In their play children learn at their highest level. Play with peers is important for children's development.
1.2 Inclusive Practice The diversity of individuals and communities is valued and respected. No child or family is discriminated against.	*2.2 Parents as Partners* Parents are children's first and most enduring educators. When parents and practitioners work together in Early Years settings, the results have a positive impact on children's development and learning.	*3.2 Supporting Every Child* The environment supports every child's learning through planned experiences and activities that are challenging but achievable.	*4.2 Active Learning* Children learn best through physical and mental challenges. Active learning involves other people, objects, ideas and events that engage and involve children for sustained periods.

Table 3.1 Continued

Theme 1: A Unique Child	Theme 2: Positive Relationships	Theme 3: Enabling Environments	Theme 4: Learning and Development
1.3 Keeping Safe Young children are vulnerable. They develop resilience when their physical and psychological well-being is protected by adults.	*2.3 Supporting Learning* Warm, trusting relationships with knowledgeable adults support children's learning more effectively than any amount of resources.	*3.3 The Learning Environment* A rich and varied environment supports children's learning and development. It gives them the confidence to explore and learn in secure and safe, yet challenging, indoor and outdoor spaces.	*4.3 Creativity and Critical Thinking* When children have opportunities to play with ideas in different situations and with a variety of resources, they discover connections and come to new and better understandings and ways of doing things. Adult support in this process enhances their ability to think critically and ask questions.
1.4 Health and Well-being Children's health is an integral part of their emotional, mental, social, environmental and spiritual well-being, and is supported by attention to these aspects.	*2.4 Key Person* A Key Person has special responsibilities for working with a small number of children, giving them the reassurance to feel safe and cared for, and building relationships with their parents.	*3.4 The Wider Context* Working in partnership with other settings, other professionals, and with individuals and groups in the community supports children's development and progress towards the outcomes of *Every Child Matters*: being healthy, staying safe, enjoying and achieving, making a positive contribution and economic well-being.	*4.4 Areas of Learning and Development* The Early Years Foundation Stage (EYFS) is made up of six areas of Learning and Development. All areas of Learning and Development are connected to one another and are equally important. All areas of Learning and Development are underpinned by the Principles of the EYFS.

Source: adapted from EYFS PiP cards (DCSF, 2008e)

- It is highly creative and flexible.

- It is free from externally applied 'rules'.

- It has active participation – mind and body.

- It has positive, often pleasurable, effects on the player(s).

- The context is open ended.

- The player is deeply involved and committed.

- The player has a real sense of decision making, ownership and control over the play.

- The player is self-directed and play often self-initiated.

Self-assessment task

Play is seen to offer children opportunities *to practise and develop new skills and competencies, to explore emotional situations, to experiment with ideas, to take risks and solve problems* (Devereux, 2010, p75).

Consider opportunities for children's play in your setting. Record the activities and experiences you provide to enable children to accomplish the following play qualities. How do they link to children's learning?

- Experiment with people and things.

- Store information in his/her memory.

- Study causes and effects.

- Reason out problems.

- Build a useful vocabulary.

- Learn to control self-centred emotional reactions and impulses.

- Adapt behaviours to the cultural habits of his/her social group.

- Interpret new, and on occasion stressful, events.

- Increase ideas about self-concept.

- Develop fine and gross motor skills.
                    Source: adapted from Pugmire-Stoy (1992, p3), cited in Moyles (2007, p216)

Your familiarity with the EYFS Framework will help you to negotiate the extensive range of high-quality literature on the subject of play and young children's learning and development that was noted in Chapter 1, and there is further reading suggested at the end of this chapter.

While all practitioners working with children from birth to five years should understand the principled approach of the EYFS and apply this to their practice, it is useful to note that *what distinguishes EYPs is the depth of, and ability to apply, their knowledge and understanding . . . of the EYFS into effective personal practice* (CWDC, 2008, p14). S1, in particular, underlines the need for EYPs to be fully informed about the EYFS Framework's requirements and guidance in order to support young children's learning and development. Furthermore, it emphasises that, as a leader of Early Years practice, an EYP's knowledge and understanding of the EYFS provides them *with a common vocabulary for their work with colleagues*, which, in turn, *facilitates their support for colleagues in implementing the EYFS* (CWDC, 2008, p14).

Observation, assessment and planning

Observing children's learning and development is highly relevant to characteristics of most other EYP Standards, particularly those that fall within the groups 'Knowledge and Understanding' and 'Effective Practice' (CWDC, 2008). For example, in order to meet S10, you will be expected to *interpret the information and evidence* you obtain so that you can review *practice and provision, and . . . plan for and implement improvements* (CWDC, 2008, p28). This has implications for the development of your practice and the work on which your written tasks will be based. Observations that are made in *meaningful and purposeful contexts for the child . . . when children are deeply involved in their learning* will enable you to find out *what they really know and understand* (Drake, 2009, p214). Close observation can enable practitioners to understand much more about children's learning; as, for example, the careful documentation that incorporates *observations, notes, photographs and reflections upon children's work*, established in the pioneering practice of Reggio Emilia (Nutbrown, 2006a, p97), or the work undertaken by Goldschmied and Selleck (1996), who observed that very young babies *respond to each other with movements and vocalizations* (cited in Manning-Morton and Thorp, 2003, p75).

The EYFS recognises the significance of the process of observational assessment as a basis for informing practitioners about the provision for each child in their care. They are required to carefully observe and consider children's needs, interests, and stages of development and *use all of this information to help plan a challenging and enjoyable experience across all areas of Learning and Development* (DCSF, 2008a, p11). Planning, therefore, is a complex task; practitioners need to be alert to children's individual learning and development needs, and respond to these with a sensitive and flexible approach. As you relate your observations to inform planning for children's next steps in their learning journeys, use the questions in the practical task below to consider your process of observation.

Self-assessment task

> Observing children is simply the very best way there is of knowing where they are, where they have been and where they will go next.

> (Drummond, 2010, p43)

When you are observing children, do you think about:

- what you *see* children doing?

- what you *hear* children doing and saying?

- how you create meaning from your observations?

How does the Key Person approach support understanding of individual children in your setting?

Source: adapted from Nutbrown and Page (2008, p105)

Now reflect on your progress towards meeting S21 and consider these three key factors – associated with assessment within the EYFS – which are highlighted in the Guidance to the Standards for the award of EYPS (CWDC, 2008, p40):

- first, making systematic observations and assessments of each child's achievement, interests and learning styles;

- second, using these observations and assessments to identify learning priorities, and to plan relevant and motivating learning experiences for each child;

- third, matching observation to the expectations of the Early Learning Goals.

Creativity and critical thinking

As you observe children's play, you should also be aware of the research work on schemas (Athey, 1990, 2007; Nutbrown, 2006b). A concept of Piaget, schemas are *repeating patterns and actions that lead to the co-ordination of cognitive structures through connections and interconnections*, which can inform practitioners' support for children's learning and development *through interaction, language and the provision of relevant materials* (Wood and Attfield, 2005, p78). By making suitable provision for children's identified schema, practitioners can challenge children's thinking and extend their learning (Meade and Cubey, 2008). The work on schema theory, therefore, helps you to recognise and facilitate children's current interests and so provide the *right conditions for learning* (DCSF, 2009a, p6).

REFLECTIVE TASK

Refer back to Table 3.1 and the Guidance to the Standards for the award of Early Years Professional Status *(CWDC, 2008) so you can reflect further on EYP Standards that you think are relevant to the following statements. These statements, grouped within the four EYFS Themes, illustrate some of the ways that skilful and thoughtful practitioners support learning (DCSF, 2009a, p28). A 'best fit' approach should be adopted when undertaking this task, as individual EYP Standards, within and across groups of standards, are interrelated. You may find it helpful to share your response with a colleague, or your mentor, so that you could jointly relate these statements to actual examples of practice.*

Where possible, you should also consider any implications for the ways in which you and other practitioners support children's learning and development.

Ways in which skilled and thoughtful practitioners support learning	Links to EYP Standards

A Unique Child
- Seeking to know and understand each individual child and their development
- Showing interest and celebrating with children their interests and achievements

Positive Relationships
- Maintaining close, caring and respectful relationships
- Encouraging and supporting children to relate to others
- Supporting children to resolve their own conflicts through problem solving

Enabling Environments
- Ensuring children have sustained time to develop child-initiated activities
- Arranging, resourcing and making time for children to make free use of rich indoor and outdoor spaces
- Observing children as a natural part of all normal activity
- Interpreting children's actions and words to try to understand the child's thinking and learning
- Being sensitive to the child's thinking and learning when deciding when to interact and when to value the child's independent activity
- Joining in play and child-initiated activity following children's agendas
- Scaffolding children's learning through talk, discussing strategies and ideas, suggesting possibilities and modelling approaches
- Providing brief, well-planned, focused learning opportunities in response to observed interests, learning and development

Learning and Development
- Using daily events within the routine to provide worthwhile real-life experiences
- Varying experiences, using fresh, creative and playful approaches
- Providing first-hand experiences to explore and discover
- Directly teaching, through demonstrating or explaining
- Encouraging and supporting children to persevere through difficulties, to take risks, to ask questions and problem-solve
- Using the language of learning to focus children on themselves as learners
- Identifying and supporting next steps in learning

Source: adapted from DCSF (2009a, p27)

As you consider relevant EYP Standards in this reflective task, it is useful to remember that, during your preparation of the written tasks for your EYPS assessment, you will be applying the EYP Standards only to actual examples of *your* work and should *ensure that your claims for each standard are not superficial* (CWDC, 2009b, p23). It is important, therefore, that you develop a thorough understanding of the substance and scope of each standard so that you can demonstrate that you have met all 39 individual standards. You will also need sufficient evidence of your personal practice and leadership in each group of standards and of working across the full birth to five years age range, which includes babies, toddlers and young children (CWDC, 2009b). While your assessment is intended to be a rigorous process, you should be reassured that it is a consistent one too, and careful, professional judgement is exercised throughout the EYPS summative assessment and during subsequent moderation of assessment outcomes to determine whether candidates' claims for meeting all the EYP Standards can be upheld (CWDC, 2008).

Supporting learning

Meeting the individual needs of all children lies at the heart of the EYFS (DCSF, 2008d, p6) and this point is further emphasised in *The Children's Plan One Year On – A Progress Report*, which notes that the EYFS is *rooted in the philosophy of personalisation – helping children learn and develop at a pace which matches their unique needs* (DCSF, 2008b). As an EYP, you will need to consider whether children's individual development, interests and preferred style of learning and communication is acknowledged within your own and colleagues' provision of activities and experiences.

PRACTICAL TASK

> A substantial proportion of the content of interaction should be related to matters of actual or potential interest to the children served by the programme.
>
> *(Katz, 2010, p16)*

Reflecting on the statement above, observe and consider how practitioners in your setting recognise that children learn and develop in different ways when planning for:

- *an individual session;*
- *a week;*
- *six weeks;*
- *a year.*

Source: adapted from PiP card 4.2 (DCSF, 2008e)

Respecting each other

S27 is concerned with listening to children, which is *a vital part of establishing positive relationships with them, and is central to the process of learning and developing* (CWDC, 2008, p50). Lancaster (2006, p64) reminds us that the *United Nations Convention on the Rights of the Child (UNCRC) and UK legislation (primarily the Children Acts 1989 and 2004)* have significantly focused attention on *listening seriously to children's views, concerns and feelings.* The Mosaic Approach (Clark and Moss, 2005), which was highlighted in Chapter 1, offers Early Years practitioners the *rich potential for children to communicate and for adults to listen* (Clark, 2010, p65). It adopts a stance that children are *experts in their own lives,* and draws on an assortment of tools to *enable young children to express their ideas and feelings with confidence,* which can facilitate them to *develop new skills and competencies, which in turn, can increase their abilities to communicate with adults* (Clark, 2010, p69). The Mosaic Approach therefore could support your understanding of *children's choices and interests [which] are the driving force for building knowledge, skills and understanding* (DCSF, 2009a, p6).

Child development

It could be argued that theoretical views of children's phases of development have reinforced a view that young children have been perceived as *immature adults, many steps and stages away from the meaningful, decision-making maturity of adulthood,* and that children's *autonomy, competence, interdependence and resistance have been continually underestimated or disregarded* (Penn, 2008, p19). Indeed, more recent theoretical work has pointed to the capacities of babies and very young children *to understand a lot more than was previously thought to be the case* (Gopnik et al., 1999). The emerging view that babies *have an innate capacity from the moment they are born* challenges the perception of 'babies' ignorance' and has implications for their provision in Early Years settings (Nutbrown, 2006b, p7). Also of relevance for Early Years practitioners are findings from research on the development of synaptic connections in the brain (see Chapter 2). Though a complex, even contentious, area, brain research indicates that learning is something that *happens quite individually through the connections made within the brain as a result of some external stimulus received through the senses* and *in young children, this stimulation is play-based* (Moyles, 2007, p216).

S2 identifies that EYPs will be expected to be well informed about the broad phases of children's development from birth to the end of the EYFS, and to *also know, in general terms, the patterns of development that children typically exhibit during Key Stage 1 at school . . . and understand that some children will behave in ways that fall outside the typical range of development* (CWDC, 2008, p15). This detailed understanding of children's development, and recognition that development is influenced by cultural and environmental factors, will support your capacity to meet S7, which requires EYPs to have *high expectations of all children and commitment to ensuring that they can achieve their full potential* (CWDC, 2008, p25), and S24, which expects EYPs to *be accountable for the delivery of high quality provision* (CWDC, 2008, p43).

You may find it useful to refer to the case studies provided in *Learning, Playing and Interacting – Good Practice in the Early Years Foundation Stage*, referred to earlier in this chapter, which identify some of the ways *in which skilful and thoughtful practitioners support learning* (DCSF, 2009a, p28). These case studies have been grouped according to four of the six stages of development that are represented within the EYFS Practice Guidance (DCSF, 2008d). (The stages birth to 11 months and 8–20 months are amalgamated to form one stage of birth to 20 months, while stages 16–26 months and 22–36 months are combined to form one stage of 16–36 months.) The four age groups covered by the case studies are, therefore, closely aligned with the three age groups that are required to be covered within EYPS (birth to 20 months, 16–36 months and 30–60 months). However, as the EYFS Practice Guidance reminds us, *different children do different things at different times . . . and it is important to note that children will not necessarily progress sequentially through the stages [in the EYFS Learning and Development Guidance], since they do not represent age-related goals* (DCSF, 2008d, p11). As you consider your role as an EYP, it is also important to note that, while the complexity of activities and experiences may shift, practitioners' interactions with children should be consistently skilful and sensitive throughout all phases of development and that *the principles of observing, seeking to understand each child, and responding to support learning within a warm and trusting relationship remain the same* (DCSF, 2009a, p28).

Some useful questions precede the case studies in *Learning, Playing and Interacting – Good Practice in the Early Years Foundation Stage* (DCSF, 2009a), which could be applied not only to these accounts of practice, but more generically to examples of your own and colleagues' work to support your reflection on the development of your own personal practice and leadership and support of others. These questions have been adapted in the reflective task below, so that they can be addressed to the following case study.

CASE STUDY

Fiona, an EYP and Children's Centre manager

A group of children were building a tall tower with giant foam building blocks. Robbie and Hassan were taking turns to place a brick on top of the tower. At one of Robbie's attempts he realised he was too small to reach the top. He looked at Hassan, who was slightly taller, and asked him to keep on building the tower. Hassan added two more bricks before he too was too small. Robbie came over to me 'Look how tall our tower is; but we want it to get taller.' *I admired their tower before asking them what they could do to build a taller tower. Hassan added* 'When Robbie was too small, I could build the tower.'

'So what could you do now you're too small?' *Simultaneously they both came up with an answer: Hassan asked me to help build their tower; Robbie went and fetched a chair to stand on.*

Through a simple questioning process, which built upon the work they had already done, they each could work out solutions to their problem and ended up building a tower that was taller than myself and used up all the bricks. They were so proud of their tower that it stayed up for two days in acknowledgement of their achievements.

Self-assessment task

Reflecting on the case study above, identify how Fiona:

* observed, interpreted and responded to the children's play;

* supported and extended the children's learning;

* helped to sustain the children's play;

* supported the children's independence.

Note your answers in the table below.

Response to questions	Links to EYP Standards

Source: questions adapted from DCSF (2009a, p28)

The wider context

As an EYP, you will need to demonstrate ways in which you have developed your knowledge of effective provision for children's learning and development. This will include an understanding *not only of the curriculum that is presented but also the context within which it is presented . . . that you think is most appropriate for your setting* (Bottle, 2007, p164). It is important, therefore, to consider that your interpretation of the content of provision is influenced by *your own beliefs about how children learn, your own cultural values and what you consider are the purposes of education* (Bottle, 2007, p164). The following task enables you to consider a possible contentious issue concerning provision for children's play that may be affected by practitioners' own values and beliefs.

REFLECTIVE TASK

PiP card 4.1 suggests that practitioners should value play which is based on people such as superheroes who may mean a lot to children, even if you do not appreciate them yourself! *(DCSF, 2008e). However, Wood and Attfield (2005) note that 'rough-and-tumble' and 'superhero' play can be a contentious issue among practitioners:*

Rough-and-tumble, and superhero play often provoke energetic debates among practitioners as they strive to reconcile their personal values about what forms of play can be allowed, tolerated or banned. They often have clear ideas about what

---

is 'appropriate play' (taking into account safety factors), but at the same time struggle with their commitment to nurturing children's interests and play themes when these include play-fighting and aggression.

(Wood and Attfield, 2005, p49)

Reflecting on your own stance on 'rough-and-tumble' and 'superhero' play, consider:

- *if you and colleagues in your setting value the play of all children,* even those who tend to play noisily and often base their play on themes with which you are unfamiliar *(DCSF, 2008e);*

- *if there is a consistent approach in your setting to children's play that seems to be about fighting and power (DCSF, 2007a);*

- *how this type of play can* be facilitated, but managed in pro-social ways *in your setting (Wood and Attfield, 2005, p52).*

S33 requires you to work collaboratively and co-operatively with colleagues to enhance children's well-being, learning and development (CWDC, 2008, p64). If you are aware of any perceived difficulties about current practice or the development of provision, you will need to consider how you can resolve these areas of potential or actual conflict by working towards a shared sense of purpose and shared values so that children's learning and development can be enhanced (CWDC, 2008, p64).

The task above also enables you to consider S38, which is concerned with the EYP's continued commitment to reflect on and evaluate *the impact of their own practice on children's learning and development* and to encourage *colleagues likewise to reflect and evaluate their practice.* This process is supported by your capacity, for example, to *draw on research outcomes and other sources of effective practice as a way of informing and improving their own and colleagues' practice* or to identify your *own need for additional professional development and support colleagues to do likewise* (CWDC, 2008, p73).

Communication, Language and Literacy

The following case study illustrates how an EYP provides a 'challenging and enjoyable experience' through her interpretation of provision for Communication, Language and Literacy (CLL), one of the six areas of Learning and Development in the EYFS, shown in Table 3.2 (DCSF, 2008a, p13). You may like to consider which other areas of Learning and Development relate to the child's experience detailed in the account below.

Table 3.2 The six areas of Learning and Development in the EYFS (DCSF, 2008a)

Personal, Social and Emotional Development	Communication, Language and Literacy
Problem Solving, Reasoning and Numeracy	Knowledge and Understanding of the World
Physical Development	Creative Development

Dawn, an EYP in a community pre-school playgroup

I have always felt that my strongest area is what I contribute to children's learning experiences. I take a keen interest not only in my key children, but as we are a small setting, I am able to get to know each child well. As the rest of the staff are part time, we have an unofficial 'shared Key Person scheme'. When a child's Key Person is not in, I 'fill in for them', and so have a strong relationship with all of the children in the setting. One of my key children had a keen interest in mark making, and we would spend time together sharing this interest. He then brought me in a picture that he had done at home, I put this up in my cupboard, so that he and all the children could see it. In response, that night I made him a picture – as I knew his interests, it was of a dragon. I addressed it to him and popped it through his door on the way to work the next day. He was delighted and another one arrived for me the following week. We continued sharing this interest for some time, always at his pace (whenever he sent one, I replied, but did not initiate). As I put more words on my pictures, so did he. The feedback from his mum was extremely positive, she saw first hand the joy he got from receiving the pictures, and placed them on his wall. His mark making and emergent writing increased as he had a real purpose to use them. The bond between us increased.

I have encouraged other members of staff to show children how they value them, not necessarily to the same extent as the example above, but by becoming interested in the children and their interests. Another member of staff's key child was interested in the fire brigade. I suggested to the staff member that, in order to follow this interest, they do some research, as the child was particularly knowledgeable so that they could discuss the subject with them, and that they could both find some pictures on the internet. They then created a role play fire station together, and we arranged a visit from the fire brigade in support of this. I have strongly encouraged staff to take comprehensive notes and photographs to support this learning, for the children's files.

Part 1

In the case study above, Dawn's knowledge about what the child already knew, and her acknowledgement of the child as a competent learner, was the starting point for encouraging his learning and development (Fisher, 2008, p39). Consider how your own values and beliefs about children's learning and development influence your practice.

Part 2

In the table below, identify any EYP Standards that you think are relevant to Dawn's practice. You may find it helpful to consider, too, whether any standards you have identified are examples of personal practice or leadership and support, as candidates can replace a tick for each standard demonstrated by their written tasks with the letter 'P' (for personal practice) and the letter 'L' (for leadership and support) when completing their section of the candidate's and assessor's task and evidence grid. Though not mandatory, this method of recording can help both you and the assessor to track the nature and extent of the evidence of these two strands that run through the standards (CWDC, 2009b, p21). An example is given in the table below. While you are being encouraged to think of linked EYP Standards in the above task, however, it is important to note that you should avoid the temptation to use a single written task to try and demonstrate the majority or all the standards (CWDC, 2009b, p20).

Example of practice	Links to EYP Standards demonstrating Personal practice (P) or Leadership and support (L)
Another member of staff's key child was interested in the fire brigade. I suggested to the staff member that, in order to follow this interest, they do some research, as the child was particularly knowledgeable so that they could discuss the subject with them, and that they could both find some pictures on the internet.	S1 (L) S12 (L) S16 (L) S25 (L) S33 (L) S37 (L)

Children's learning and development

When interacting with the child, his parent and other staff in her setting in the task above, it could be said that Dawn had considered *the* what*, who and* hows *of learning, which are 'crucially interlinked'* (Anning and Edwards, 2010, p8). This viewpoint highlights the traditional prominence assigned within Early Years provision to the developmental perspective of *how* children learn, to include a focus on supporting children to perceive themselves as learners. This emphasis on dispositional learning has been a key factor within Early Years provision in New Zealand, where dispositions are referred to *as 'habits of mind' and 'patterns of learning' which provide the foundation for future independent learning* (Anning and Edwards, 2010, p8). As you provide support for children's learning and development in your setting, you could therefore consider:

- *what* children are learning;
- *how* children become people *who* are learners;
- *how* children learn;
- *how* their learning is supported.

(adapted from Anning and Edwards, 2010)

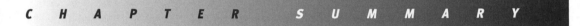

C H A P T E R   S U M M A R Y

This chapter has focused on aspects of children's learning and development relevant to the role of an EYP, who is supporting and leading practice across the EYFS. Young children's learning and development, though, is an extensive and dynamic subject – and one that is intrinsically related to notions of childhood itself, and views about content and contexts for learning. This has implications for you, as an EYP, in terms of your provision for children's learning and development, as *practitioners create their own knowledge about what works, taking into account the complex contextual variables in their settings* (Wood and Attfield, 2005, p58).

Moving on

Aspects of Early Years practice that have been covered in this chapter are developed elsewhere in this book. In the next chapter, we consider further how EYPs work with parents and colleagues to meet the needs of all children in their settings in order to promote their learning and development.

FURTHER READING

DCSF (2008f) *Young Brains*, on EYFS CD-ROM. Nottingham: DCSF.

DCSF (2009a) *Learning, Playing and Interacting – Good Practice in the Early Years Foundation Stage (The National Strategies/Early Years)*. Nottingham: DCSF.

Miller, L, Cable, C and Goodliff, G (eds) (2010) *Supporting Children's Learning in the Early Years* (2nd edn). London: Routledge.

Wood, E and Attfield, J (2005) *Play, Learning and the Early Childhood Curriculum.* London: Paul Chapman.

4 Meeting the needs of all children

CHAPTER OBJECTIVES

This chapter considers how Early Years Professionals (EYPs) ensure all children are included in their Early Years setting, and explores ways in which positive attitudes to diversity and difference are promoted, as required by the Early Years Foundation Stage (EYFS) (DCSF, 2008a). Inclusive practice is concerned with practitioners' attitudes and behaviours, and this chapter explores how EYPs can lead and support others to build trusting relationships between children and their families, to ensure that they feel welcomed, valued and respected. While a detailed exploration of individual needs that children might present is beyond the scope of this chapter, focused case studies are offered to facilitate a consideration of strategies that could be employed to support inclusive practice.

After reading this chapter you should be able to:
- consider how you respect and value all children with whom you work;
- develop strategies to build positive relationships that support children's learning, development and well-being;
- reflect critically on how you promote positive attitudes to diversity and difference.

Though reference is made to many of the EYP Standards, S4, S5, S6, S7, S12, S18, S25, S27 and S29–36 are particularly relevant to this chapter.

Introduction

In Chapter 3, we explored the significance of listening to children when supporting their learning and development. We referred to S27, which sets out the need for EYPs to *respect children and believe that children of all ages, backgrounds and abilities are important, unique and worth listening to* (CWDC, 2008, p50). This expectation is also highly applicable to the focus of this chapter, which is concerned with meeting the needs of all children, which *lies at the heart of the EYFS* (DCSF, 2008d, p7).

This chapter considers the need for EYPs to form positive relationships with children by focusing on their individual needs, appreciating their skills, preferences and interests, and treating them with fairness, respect and consideration (S25, CWDC, 2008, p48). Fair and respectful treatment of children is implicit in the EYFS Commitment 1.2, *Inclusive Practice*, which states that all children have rights and entitlements and that *no child or family is discriminated against* (DCSF, 2008e).

We also consider S18, which expects EYPs to actively promote equality of opportunity and anti-discriminatory practice, as these are crucial actions for improving outcomes for children (CWDC, 2008, p36). By thinking about the individual, as well as the collective needs of children, EYPs promote an open, safe and secure environment, and ensure all children feel welcomed, included and valued in the setting. EYPs encourage other practitioners to develop positive relationships with children too, so that they can build a better understanding of individual children, rather than make assumptions about them. One of the ways that EYPs address children's individual interests and needs is through the selection and use of resources that provide opportunities and experiences for children, and support their learning and development (see S12). Chosen resources should positively reflect *the ethnic, social, cultural and religious diversity in society* (CWDC, 2008, p30).

The significance of EYPs' partnership work with parents, colleagues and other professionals across children's services, which is a central element of S29–36, is also explored. By using effective communication, EYPs engage all parties involved in Early Years provision for young children, both within and beyond the setting. We therefore consider how EYPs communicate sensitively and effectively with parents, especially in difficult situations (S30) and work collaboratively and co-operatively with colleagues to promote children's well-being, learning and development (S33).

EYPs also provide support for children and their families by engaging in partnership work with other Early Years practitioners and professionals, and share relevant information with them, according to agreed procedures (S6, S36). An EYP's approach to practice must be informed by a sound and current understanding of Early Years national and local frameworks, policies and guidance, as well as relevant legal requirements (S4, S5). This knowledge supports EYPs' subsequent review and modification of practice, as well as the implementation of any new policies (S35). You will find further information on policy documents, legislation and guidance on practice relating to equitable and inclusive practice at the end of this chapter.

Promoting equality for all children

Equality for all children is a central requirement for Early Years settings; the EYFS expects that:

> *all children, irrespective of ethnicity, culture, or religion, home language, family back-ground, learning difficulties or disabilities, gender or ability should have the opportunity to experience a challenging and enjoyable programme of learning and development.*
> (DCSF, 2008a, p10)

This requirement, which is premised on UK and European legislation and policies designed to combat discrimination and protect children's rights, is incorporated into S18 (CWDC, 2008). This standard expects EYPs to promote, facilitate, monitor and evaluate equality practices in their setting. Policies and procedures should, therefore, be underpinned by principles of equality (Lane, 2008) to ensure that children's rights are upheld and that the Early Years setting includes all children.

S18 also expects EYPs to maintain an updated working knowledge on the dynamic area of legislation, policy and practice relating to the responsibilities of their role in Early Years settings (CWDC, 2008). By keeping abreast of current research pertaining to Early Years practice (S38) EYPs demonstrate they are responsive to changes in practice, which seek to improve outcomes for children (S39) (CWDC, 2008). For example, the government introduced the social change campaign, 'Think Fathers', in November 2008, which aimed to promote public understanding about fatherhood. EYPs might, therefore, seek to explore ways in which all practitioners in the setting could actively engage children's fathers and be supportive of father–child relationships (DCSF, 2008g).

A further EYP Standard that should be considered in this chapter is S7, which requires EYPs to be committed to ensuring that all children can achieve their full potential; this standard expects EYPs, for instance, *to challenge stereotypical views of what children can achieve* (CWDC, 2008, p25). Promoting equality for every child in your setting can present its challenges and you will find some examples of situations that practitioners may face on EYFS PiP Card 1.2 (DCSF, 2008e). In the following case study, we consider how an EYP took positive steps to effectively support a child's well-being, learning and development.

CASE STUDY

Fiona, an EYP and Children's Centre manager

One of the key aspects involved in my practice relates to inclusion and equality within the setting. On one occasion a child, Harry, was registered to attend the pre-school. During his settling-in period it was evident that there were additional needs which we would need to consider were we to give him equal access to the group. His parents were in denial regarding his level of needs and hoped it was 'something that he would grow out of'. Within the first few weeks, with permission from his parents, I arranged meetings with the Area SENCO, organised support funding and trained a staff member as a one-to-one support worker.

As Harry settled, with the aid of his worker, we looked into longer-term provision for his needs as it became evident through observations that there was the possibility of Harry being on the autistic spectrum, with routines and language being two key areas for future development. I organised for his one-to-one support worker and parents to attend visual timetable* training, which helped organise Harry's physical day in a meaningful context for him; we found that this had an immediate effect on his behaviour and concentration during activities. As his language development was delayed I organised Makaton** training for the whole staff team and his parents. As the same process was in place during his core day and at home it ensured consistency to approaching Harry's language development and, within a year, he had progressed considerably from no detectable words to short phrases.

Our long-term efforts rested upon gaining a statement for Harry to ensure that he was suitably supported when he moved to school; this was a long process which I co-ordinated between the Educational Psychologist, Speech and Language Therapist, Area SENCO and Pre-School Teacher. Harry is now in Year 2 of a mainstream primary with a one-to-one support worker for 50 per cent of his school day. He integrates with the rest of his class and communicates at a recognisable level. His one-to-one support worker and I are still in regular contact with his parents who update us on his progress. Harry is a distinct example as it illustrates the whole process of ensuring that not only the child, but the parents and staff are supported in achieving the best learning outcomes for the child.

* Visual timetables help to decrease a child's confusion or distress that could arise by not knowing what will happen next (DCSF, 2009b).

** Makaton is a system of communication that involves signs and speech to support a child's understanding. Further information about this system can be found on the *Every Child Matters* website. Details of this website and more information on supporting children with autism are included at the end of this chapter.

REFLECTIVE TASK

Reflecting on the case study above, consider the following questions.

- *What challenges did Fiona encounter when supporting Harry?*

- *How did Fiona provide effective support for Harry?*

- *Who was involved in providing this support?*

- *Which EYP Standards are relevant to this case study?*

The further reading included at the end of this chapter contains some useful material that supports reflection on inclusive practice, and case studies that illustrate further examples of effective provision for supporting young children's individual needs and ensuring their sense of well-being. For example, the case studies in *Supporting Children on the Autistic Spectrum: Guidance for Practitioners in the Early Years Foundation Stage* (DCSF, 2009b) are particularly relevant to the case study above.

A challenge to the development of inclusive practice can occur where practitioners are resistant to the policy requirements intended to ensure equality and inclusion in their setting. Jones (2004) contends that overcoming such resistance to inclusive practice requires a culture that recognises the normality of diversity. EYPs should therefore ensure that positive attitudes to diversity and difference are adopted by both practitioners and children themselves. This will serve not only to ensure that every child is included in everyday practice but also that they learn to value diversity themselves (DCSF, 2008a).

When considering how to promote equality in Early Years settings, it is useful to examine how our own experiences affect and shape our views and beliefs. Our attitudes to difference have a significant influence over our practice and we may find ourselves seeking to be more supportive of some children than others, whether this is intentional or not (Lane, 2008). It is important, therefore, for EYPs to reflect on their own perspectives on difference and diversity as openly as possible when seeking to establish inclusive practice.

The following practical task encourages you to think about how you have applied strategies that promote inclusion and equality in your setting, and then to consider how your values and beliefs impacted on these strategies. If you cannot provide an actual example from practice, you could suggest how you would apply the strategy in your setting.

Self-assessment task

Considering examples of how you have applied the strategies listed below will enable you to examine how your values and beliefs can influence your perceptions of different groups of children. An example has been provided for the first strategy, but you are encouraged to include one of your own as well.

Strategies to promote inclusive practice within an Early Years setting	An example from your practice of how you have applied this strategy	Thoughts about your underlying values and beliefs that may have influenced your practice
Encourage everyday experiences of people in the local community to be shared within the setting	*Displayed narratives of everyday lives of members of families in the local community, which were shared in a manner and place in the setting that was accessible to all* Your example:	*Individuals from different community groups should be recognised and appreciated equally to encourage their sense of belonging in a setting* Your thoughts:
Ensure planned activities acknowledge children's own experiences and needs		
Ensure children's use of home languages is valued and supported		
Encourage children to think about issues of gender, class and culture		

Strategies to promote inclusive practice within an Early Years setting	An example from your practice of how you have applied this strategy	Thoughts about your underlying values and beliefs that may have influenced your practice
Counter negative attitudes expressed about different individuals or groups within the setting and beyond		
Ensure resources enable participation, and support the learning of all children		
Ensure resources promote positive images of different groups of children and counter stereotypical perceptions		
Involve practitioners in formulating and evaluating equality policies in the setting		
Provide opportunities for consultation with parents about the setting's equality policies		

You may wish to discuss the outcomes of this task with a colleague, mentor or tutor, and jointly reflect on how your values and beliefs have impacted on your provision. Such joint reflection may be helpful in demonstrating how our own experiences affect and shape our views and beliefs. This, in turn, impacts upon our understanding of diverse groups of children and their families, and the inclusiveness of our practice.

Special Educational Needs Co-ordinators (SENCOs)

All settings registered with Ofsted should have a designated person, known as a Special Educational Needs Co-ordinator (SENCO) or sometimes an Inclusion Co-ordinator (INCO), who is responsible for implementing the setting's SEN policy and overseeing inclusive practice. The SENCO may, for example, support the early identification of children's individual needs, enabling families and professionals to access additional support associated with a child's disability or emerging special educational needs, through the *Early Support* programme (DfES, 2006).

Though EYPs may not hold the role of SENCO in their setting, they should support colleagues to assess individual children's needs and ensure children feel both emotionally and physically safe. For example, EYPs should seek to identify and support children who have been affected by changes or difficulties in their personal lives, and recognise when and how to refer children to colleagues for specialist support, as required by S23 (CWDC, 2008). They may also indicate to parents where they can receive extra support or advice – for instance, about their child's speech, language and communication development (DCSF, 2008h). By being approachable and providing a welcoming atmosphere, EYPs can encourage parents to exchange information about their child's well-being, learning and development (S32).

Integrated working

Additionally, EYPs may work with other Early Years providers and key professionals to provide integrated support for children (S36) (CWDC, 2008). Integrated working is a process that is central to the *Every Child Matters* agenda (DfES, 2004); it requires everyone who is involved in supporting a child to work together effectively. Integrated working places the child at the centre of the process. By collaborating and co-ordinating their efforts, professionals can combine their expertise, knowledge and skills to achieve better outcomes for children. EYPs should develop and sustain a culture that supports integrated working practices, and ensure they communicate effectively with other professionals. The *2020 Children and Young People's Workforce Strategy* (CYPWS) highlighted that integrated working is an important feature of early intervention, which seeks to ensure children and their families receive timely support (DCSF, 2008g).

By drawing on their skills and experiences, EYPs can also contribute towards the Common Assessment Framework (CAF). This is a standardised approach to assessing children's additional needs, which are not being met by their access to current provision of services. Co-ordinated support to address these needs can be identified through the CAF. As an EYP, you may be involved in sharing information between practitioners from different sectors to support the delivery of services identified within an individual child's CAF.

You may encounter some obstacles when working collaboratively with other professionals, such as a different use of terminology when bringing forward information for the CAF. These potential barriers will need to be effectively managed to ensure that children can benefit from integrated services and receive support tailored to their individual needs. Where more than one agency is involved in meeting identified needs of a child, one practitioner, known as the Lead Professional, undertakes a leading role (CWDC, 2009c). This individual is responsible for co-ordinating the provision of support from different professionals for children with additional needs and also acts as a single point of contact for those children and their families.

Self-assessment task

You are encouraged to reflect on the following two questions that are concerned with the policy of Integrated Working.

1. To what extent could you explain to a parent how the CAF could support their child's needs?

2. How is information about children and families shared securely and effectively within and beyond your setting?

Further information on Integrated Working, the Common Assessment Framework and the Lead Professional is available on the Every Child Matters website, details of which are included at the end of this chapter.

Positive relationships

We considered S25 at the beginning of this chapter; it describes the supportive and constructive relationships EYPs form with young children (CWDC, 2008). As an EYP, you will need to ensure that all children and their families feel welcomed and valued, by acknowledging their different needs and expectations. This enables children to feel supported, confident and safe within the Early Years setting, so that they develop a sense of belonging and are willing to try new experiences. EYPs must also be aware of the role and significance of the Key Person in developing positive relationships with their assigned children. The Key Person approach is explained in EYFS Commitment 2.3 (DCSF, 2008e), which encourages practitioners to develop a genuine bond with children, accommodate their individual needs, and provide them with consistent care and emotional support (Elfer *et al.*, 2003). The role of the Key Person is discussed in detail in Chapter 6.

The following case study describes how an EYP, Sajal, who is an outreach worker in a Children's Centre, has provided opportunities for children to feel more confident and secure when they come to the Centre.

CASE STUDY

Sajal, an EYP who is an outreach worker in a Children's Centre

When the new children have come in for settling I have established a positive relationship with the parents that has helped them to feel less anxious so that they feel comfortable leaving their children at the Centre. As many of the new parents have been very anxious leaving their children for the first time I have done many home visits beforehand so that when they eventually come into the Centre they have a familiar face to work with. This has really helped us and the new parents to get to know the children in a better aspect. If needs be, we first invite them to the 'play and stay' group before they start in the actual rooms. I found this really helps the children to feel more settled.

REFLECTIVE TASK

- *Successful transitions enable children to feel a similar sense of well-being and belonging in both their home and Early Years setting. Reflecting on the case study above, consider how Sajal ensured that children felt secure when they came to the centre. Note any EYP Standards that you think are relevant to this case study.*

REFLECTIVE TASK *continued*

- *Now consider how you manage transitions sensitively in your setting. How do you ensure that children and their families really feel welcomed in the setting? Again, note any EYP Standards you feel would be relevant to your example.*

The importance of children's feelings should be acknowledged when considering the provision for all children in the Early Years setting. You will need to consider, for example, how a child may feel if they are presented with different routines. It is increasingly recognised that emotions can promote or impede learning, and that links between children's feelings and early brain development are particularly critical during the early stages of their lives (Dowling, 2010). This view is supported by Stroh *et al.* (2008, p20), who describe how neuro-science research has shown an important connection between emotional and cognitive functions. It is useful, therefore, to consider in the practical task below some ways in which you support children's emotional well-being.

PRACTICAL TASK

You will need to refer to the requirements for Personal, Social and Emotional Development, one of the six areas of learning and development within the EYFS (DCSF, 2008a) to carry out this task.

As you read through these requirements, identify some corresponding examples of suitable provision for each of the actions identified in the table below, which would enable children to feel safe and secure. Record in the right-hand column the EYP Standards that relate to your examples.

Actions	Your corresponding example	Relevant EYP Standards
Ensure that children feel physically and emotionally safe	*Provide a second Key Person so there is a familiar person available for a child to trust when their main key worker is absent*	*S13, S19*
	Your example:	Your example:
Recognise that children need territorial space		

PRACTICAL TASK continued

Actions	Your corresponding example	Relevant EYP Standards
Acknowledge that children feel they belong through having routines and rituals		
Help children to label and recognise their feelings		
Assist children to learn strategies to calm down		
Help children to cope with their fears and anxieties		

Source: adapted from DCSF (2008i, p16)

You are also encouraged to reflect on how you can support a child who is finding it difficult to manage their feelings. How would you ensure that there is a consistent approach to supporting this child?

English as an additional language

The importance of home languages is emphasised in the EYFS guidance, *Supporting Children Learning English as an Additional Language* (EAL), which affirms that bilingualism should be regarded as an asset (DCSF, 2007b). Language is a vital part of a child's identity and has a continuing role in their learning and acquisition of additional languages; however, we should also recognise that *EAL children are not a homogenous group* and *their needs will be individual* (DCSF, 2007b, p7). Practitioners should note that effective strategies to support all children, such as the use of visual clues, also provide relevant support for children with EAL (DCSF, 2008h). Some key features of practice that effectively support second language acquisition are listed below:

- maintenance of the children's home language;

- an ethos that builds self-esteem and celebrates the individual;

- reflection of the cultural/ethnic and religious differences in activities, stories, resources and pictures;

- a strong partnership with parents;

- planned opportunities for talk with and between children;

- provision of good models of standard spoken and written English;

- recognition and understanding of the stages of second language acquisition;

- introduction to new vocabulary in meaningful contexts;

- the use of rhyme, rhythm and repetition in stories and songs;

- the use of regular, repeated routines throughout the day to foster a sense of security about the nature and purpose of activities.

Source: Marsh and Hallet (2008, p25)

The second statement in the list above concerns the development of self-esteem. Developing a high level of self-esteem and a clear sense of identity is essential for a child's development of resilience, which enables them to tackle the more challenging experiences in life. Good relationships with their Key Person and other practitioners in the setting will support a child's confidence when attempting to confront challenges, and will also help them not to be afraid of failing or being ridiculed (DCSF, 2008e).

PRACTICAL TASK

Observe and reflect on how the current practice in your setting supports children's development of a positive self-identity and self-esteem. Then consider your response to each of the questions in the table below.

Question about the current provision in your setting	Response
How do adults and children relate to each other?	
What does the setting feel like to its users?	
Which aspects of the existing provision are positive?	
Which aspects of the existing provision are negative?	
Who is responsible for change?	

Source: adapted from Siraj-Blatchford (2006, p113)

These questions cover important aspects of practice that are relevant to developing positive relationships with all children and their families. By focusing on the practice in

PRACTICAL TASK *continued*

your setting, you can gain a better understanding of the impact of everyday experience in the setting for children, parents and staff, as well as others who may visit the setting. It is also useful to review whether staff adopt a similar approach when respecting and valuing all children who attend the setting. Effective communication between different settings or family members who are involved with the child's development is important too.

The role of story

The use of story is included in the list of key features of practice that were considered earlier in this chapter. Marsh and Hallet (2008, p97) emphasise the particular significance of story to young children's *personal, linguistic and conceptual development*. The importance of listening to stories was previously highlighted in Gordon Wells' seminal longitudinal study of children's language and literacy development in Bristol. This research noted that, through the experience of story, children began to discover the *symbolic potential of language; its power to create possible or imaginary worlds through words* (Wells, 1987, p156). Wells identified that the symbols used to represent certain relationships, events or objects could be interpreted in other contexts than those in which the experience originally took place.

An example of how story can be used to promote *all* children's understanding and use of language is detailed in the case study below; this account additionally demonstrates how an EYP supported another practitioner in the setting with their provision of storytelling.

CASE STUDY

Theresa, an EYP in a pre-school playgroup, describes her experience of storytelling

I have encouraged and invited all staff to engage in small group circle times (music and movement, stories, songs and rhymes, number time, sharing stories/experiences), by ensuring colleagues buddy up with each other to offer support. When I have read stories, I have written reflective accounts on occasion, as examples of good practice to share with colleagues, identifying learning goals, etc. I have also encouraged other colleagues to do likewise when I have seen examples of good practice. For example, on a windy day, a colleague read a story about a kite, which I then suggested was expanded to include a larger group at circle time, using our own kite as a visual prop. My colleague also then included dressing-up items, hats, jackets, other props, to give to children as they became various characters in the story, holding on to the kite string. Later, the children went out to play in the garden to fly the kite, blow bubbles, hold ribbons and feel the windy weather for themselves. I asked my colleagues to keep a reflective account of this sustained learning over the day.

REFLECTIVE TASK

Part 1

Reflecting on the case study above, consider how Theresa:

- *advised on* the provision of a range of resources to support children's language and communication *(S15) (CWDC, 2008, p33);*

- *worked* collaboratively and co-operatively with colleagues to enhance children's well-being, learning and development *(S33) (CWDC, 2008, p64);*

- *led and supported* colleagues in the review of and evaluation of practice *(S34) (CWDC, 2008, p65).*

Part 2

Select a story that you think is suitable for the needs of the children with whom you currently work. Then consider how you would enable all children to access this story – for example, by providing story props or visual support (Smidt, 2009). Ensure these resources avoid negative stereotypes and are representative of children's diverse backgrounds. Note any EYP Standards that you think are relevant to this task.

You may find it helpful to refer to a case study about the use of story in Building Futures: Believing in Children – A Focus on Provision for Black Children in the Early Years Foundation Stage, *which describes the use of the text* So Much *(Cooke, 1994). The practitioners in this case study had chosen this story to recognise the specific linguistic and cultural heritages of families who were attending the nursery (DCSF, 2009c, p34).*

Think about how the use of stories could be developed in your setting, when leading and supporting provision for the development of speech, language and communication skills for all children. You might also reflect on the following suggested actions:

- *ensure there is a strategy for the development of speech, language and communication that includes details of how children who do not have well-developed skills, or have speech, language and communication needs, are being identified and supported;*

- *develop a strategy that is understood by all practitioners, and is implemented, reviewed and continually improved;*

- *include the development of children's vocabulary in the strategy, and ensure that all practitioners understand their role in this;*

- *give time and support for practitioners to develop the skills needed for them to engage in sustained shared thinking;*

- *regularly analyse the children's progress and achievements in speech, language and communication, share this analysis with all practitioners, implement reviews of practice, and support improvements.*

Source: DCSF (2008h, p57)

Resources

S12 is concerned with an appropriate choice and use of resources that positively reflects *the ethnic, social, cultural and religious diversity in society* (CWDC, 2008, p30). However, while resources may seem interesting and attractive, we need to recognise that *the choice of resources alone will not ensure equality and inclusion; it is the way in which they are used that will promote both* (CWDC, 2008, p30). Therefore, it is useful to also consider *how* resources are used effectively. EYPs should regularly reflect on how resources are used, and evaluate their effectiveness for all children in the setting. For example, you may wish to review whether all children understand practitioners' instructions about the safe use of resources or if they are all encouraged to engage in messy play, if they initially seem reluctant to participate in the activity. The use of resources is discussed further in Chapter 5, but it is useful here to consider the use of a resource that can promote positive attitudes to difference and include all children.

Use of resources: persona dolls

Persona dolls are a physical learning resource for practitioners. Each doll has an individual name, family and personality, which represents both children and adults from diverse backgrounds. They are used to tell stories concerning equality issues, and promote the sharing of children's thoughts and feelings (Brown, 1998). Research has demonstrated that the use of persona dolls, which provides a powerful method of storytelling, can effectively support equality work with children (Van Keulen, 2004). The opportunity to tell stories with a doll, rather than read them, enables practitioners to adapt the stories more readily to children's individual needs. The stories are set within contexts, which could, for example, highlight unfair or unkind behaviours that have been directed towards one of the dolls. The children are then encouraged to express their feelings towards the doll's plight and consider appropriate actions that could rectify this situation. In seeking to find a way to help the dolls, children gain experience of more positive attitudes, thereby supporting their development of empathy towards others. Further information on the use of persona dolls is provided at the end of this chapter. The case study below details practice involving the use of a persona doll to address a specific issue that had arisen in an EYP's setting.

CASE STUDY

Allana, an EYP and manager in a private nursery

I had recently attended persona doll training, where I had been given the opportunity to see and use these dolls as a powerful resource. Following this training I acquired a persona doll and named him Marcus.

Within the setting a young boy was finding it difficult to make friends because of his often challenging behaviour and his tendency to hit out at others. During story time, and modelling this for other practitioners, I introduced Marcus to the children by talking about his family and home life. I explained that Marcus had come to visit to ask for the

---

children's help. He wanted to make new friends but was not sure how to do this; sometimes Marcus did not like to share his toys and sometimes he would get cross and shout, and this made people sad.

I asked the children if they had any ideas to help Marcus. Lots of the children were keen to make suggestions and offered to share their toys with Marcus and to be his friend. Many children were able to share their ideas about how sad Marcus might be feeling.

In the following sessions, children brought items in from home to share with Marcus, including the child with challenging behaviour, and Marcus was included in children's games within the setting.

One child brought her mum into the setting to meet her new friend and Marcus also received an invitation to a birthday party, which he attended with great excitement.

Over a period of weeks Marcus visited on numerous occasions and the child with behavioural difficulties began to be more included by others, who showed more tolerance towards him as his angry outbursts became less frequent.

As other staff had been interested to learn more about persona dolls I organised for someone very experienced in using this resource to come in and provide training for interested practitioners, and cascaded knowledge and understanding from my own experience too.

Marcus and one of his friends are frequent visitors to the setting, sharing their many experiences, and are always warmly welcomed by the children.

Self-assessment task

Part 1

From your reading of the case study, consider how Allana's use of the persona doll in her setting encouraged the children to think positively about difference. Then reflect on ways in which you have promoted positive views of difference in your work with children. Identify any actions that you think were particularly successful.

Part 2

Now reflect on how you would encourage other practitioners to support children to develop their capacity to empathise with others. This is dependent on an understanding that:

- our feelings are important to us;
- other people have feelings;
- others may think and feel differently from us.

Practitioners can support the development of empathy by:

- encouraging secure attachment by getting to know each child and their parents, being available at the beginning of the day and being 'tuned in' to their needs and feelings;

- demonstrating active listening, and modelling awareness of the feelings of others;

- encouraging children to listen to each other and notice each other's feelings;

- providing opportunities to develop the skills of empathy, and modelling those skills themselves.

Source: adapted from DCSF (2008i, p17)

Partnerships with parents

There is considerable evidence to support the view that effective partnerships with parents can have a positive impact on children's learning and development (Siraj-Blatchford *et al.*, 2002a; Whalley *et al.*, 2007; DCSF, 2008e). However, while most parents wish to be involved in their child's provision, some find it difficult (DCSF, 2009d). You may, for example, encounter reluctance on the part of some families to consistently engage with the provision on offer or to readily communicate with staff in your setting. It is important to consider how you can build respectful partnerships with parents who may seem less inclined to be involved.

REFLECTIVE TASK

Consider the following questions, which support a joint understanding of professional and parental views, and try to determine where there is convergence and divergence *in* beliefs, values, assumptions and practices *(McDermott, 2008, p131).*

- *What is the work environment of the parent? Is it restrictive? Allowing for autonomy? Supportive? Entrepreneurial?*

- *Do the parents experience high or low degrees of role strain?*

- *Do the parents feel supported by each other, family, friends, community and the setting?*

- *Do the parents have an opportunity to observe other parents or caregivers interacting with their children?*

- *Are you as a professional taking into consideration parental factors such as family and other social supports?*

- *What about the number and perception of stressful life events in the family?*

- *Do the parents feel the neighbourhood, state and government have responsibilities to help the child or family? What do the parents do when this support does not materialise?*

- *How do the parents' neighbourhoods affect their parenting?*

- *How are marital relations or relations with a partner affecting their parenting?*

- *Are enough mental and physical health resources available for the parents?*

- *Do the parents have a sense of self-efficacy in their various roles?*

Source: adapted from McDermott (2008, p130)

McDermott further highlights the need to learn what parental involvement means in different cultures and to understand the goals of parents, which may differ from the stereotypes of their cultural group (McDermott, 2008, p132). Seeking to identify possible barriers to parents engaging more effectively with their child's setting will, in turn, enable EYPs to work out strategies for removing these barriers and work with parents for the benefit of the child.

The Pen Green Centre for Under Fives in Corby has developed a model that represents dialogue about a child between staff at the centre and the significant adult(s) in the child's home. Parents are asked to share their observations of their children at home with staff at the Centre, which can then inform the staff's provision for the child. Staff, too, share their observations with parents, and so can influence the child's provision at home. This is particularly important given that *what parents do with their children at home . . . is much more significant than any other factor open to educational influence* (Desforges with Abouchaar, 2003, p91). The model shown in Figure 4.1 demonstrates the working of the Pen Green Loop.

The benefits of partnership working between parents and staff at the Pen Green Centre are listed below.

- Parents benefit from increasing their knowledge and understanding of their children through group discussion with other parents and staff.

- Staff benefit through increasing their knowledge and understanding of their children's learning opportunities at home; their ability to provide continuity and new experiences for the child within the nursery is then extended.

- Children benefit because the significant adults in their lives are able to provide richer learning opportunities.

- Children also experience their parents and carers working closely together. This gives them a sense of continuity and being cared for, and creates a trusting and secure environment in which they can learn and grow.

Source: Whalley *et al.* (2007)

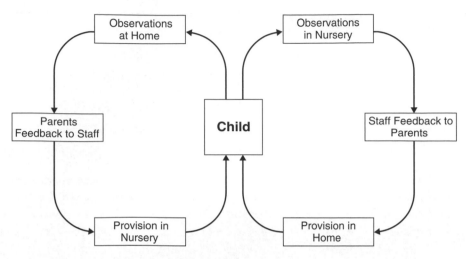

Figure 4.1 Model of the Pen Green Loop

Source: Whalley *et al.* (2007)

The following case study demonstrates how Dawn, an EYP in a Community Pre-school Playgroup, supported a child in her setting. Dawn recognised that she needed to engage with a child's parents in order to gain *a more complete picture* of the child's life and so provide more effective support, as described in her account below.

Dawn, an EYP in a community pre-school playgroup

By treating each family's needs individually we have been able to ensure that each child and family has been supported throughout their time with us. A girl attended two days with us and went to another setting for two days. She had not had a positive experience at her other setting at lunchtime, and each lunchtime became very distressed. I talked at length with her parents to discover exactly what was wrong. She had a very limited diet as she would not eat or try many foods. The nursery where she attended cooked on site and refused for her to take a pack-up. They insisted that she ate the nursery food and, when she didn't, insisted that she remain at the table. She built up a huge anxiety around sitting with a group of children. She was able to bring a pack-up with us, however due to her previous experience was not able to sit with the other children. I offered to her and her parents that she could sit with me, as I sat away from the other children to have my lunch (other staff covered the lunchtime). Each day we sat away quietly and slowly she began to build her confidence, I chatted to her over lunch, and was led completely by her, as to what and how much she wanted to eat. She had always spent quite a lot of her time within the session with me, and for a little while, she spent most of her time with me. However, eventually her confidence began to grow, first during the session, she would go off and play with other children. After a considerable amount of time, and slowly moving our table nearer and nearer to where the other children had lunch, then both of us sitting

---

CASE STUDY *continued*

in, she finally joined the children without my support. Such a small commitment from me enabled her to spend the whole day in the group with us with her peers. As she joined school the feedback I got from mum was that she settled straight into having lunch with very few concerns.

I have always stressed the importance to other staff members of treating each family as an individual, and meeting their needs is paramount to ensure that each child is settled, happy and secure within the group. We spend a considerable amount of time discussing children's needs at staff meetings, to ensure they are all met, thus ensuring each child and family is included, valued, respected and feels that they are treated equally.

Some of the children sometimes asked why the child was sitting with me at lunch, and staff sensitively explained that she sometimes felt a little bit upset and so I was looking after her. As she began to join them, they took on the caring role and would offer 'M can sit with me today, I will look after her.' This supported our ethos of caring and looking after one another.

PRACTICAL TASK

Part 1

Reflect on the case study above and consider how Dawn enabled the child to be included in her setting. Now provide a response to the questions in the table below, in respect of the case study.

Question	Response
What were the initial barriers to inclusion?	
What actions did Dawn undertake to support the child?	
Who did she involve?	
Which EYP Standards are relevant to her actions?	
How did Dawn lead and support other practitioners?	

Part 2

Explore any EYP Standards that you think are relevant to the features of practice included in the table below. These features show how effective settings communicate with parents, as partners in children's learning.

Features of successful settings' work with parents	Relevant EYP Standards
Encourage high levels of parental engagement in their children's learning, work hard to build trust and help parents to see they have a role	
Staff have responsibility for parental involvement – establish clear strategies and evaluate impact	
Share educational aims and practice with parents – and work to develop mutual understandings	
Value information from parents and share information about individual children regularly (some on a monthly or even weekly basis)	
Encourage parents to support children at home with activities and materials that complement those used at the setting	
Work proactively to remove barriers to collaboration – making everyone feel welcome	
Make efforts to know the wider community well and where other sources of support for families are located	

Source: adapted from Resource Sheet 6.3, PEAL Reader (in Wheeler and Connor, 2009)

C H A P T E R   S U M M A R Y

This chapter has explored the multifaceted area of provisions for individual children's needs. We have explored how equality and inclusive practice aims to support and include all children, and how integrated working practices can provide effective support to meet children's specific individual needs. This is dependent on effective and respectful communication among professionals who are involved in supporting children's individual needs, and between those professionals and the children and families whom they serve.

Moving on

In the next chapter, we consider the significance of the emotional environment in Early Years settings, and explore issues relating to the provision of a safe, stimulating and challenging indoor and outdoor environment. By referring to relevant EYP Standards and the EYFS Framework, we will explore the impact of the environment on children's learning, development and well-being.

FURTHER READING

DCSF (2010) *Finding and Exploring Young Children's Fascinations: Strengthening the Quality of Gifted and Talented Provision in the Early Years.* Nottingham: DCSF.

The National Strategy publications listed below are available to download from the following website: www.standards.dcsf.gov.uk/nationalstrategies

Confident, Capable and Creative: Supporting Boys' Achievements: Guidance for Practitioners in the Early Years Foundation Stage (DCSF, 2007a).

Supporting Children Learning English as an Additional Language: Guidance for Practitioners in the Early Years Foundation Stage (DCSF, 2007b).

Effective Practice: Inclusive Practice, available on EYFS CD-ROM, Nottingham (DCSF, 2008e).

Social and Emotional Aspects of Development: Guidance for EYFS Practitioners (DCSF, 2008i).

Inclusion Development Programme – Supporting Children with Speech, Language and Communication Needs: Guidance for Practitioners in the Early Years Foundation Stage (DCSF, 2008h).

Building Futures: Believing in Children – A Focus on Provision for Black Children in the Early Years Foundation Stage (DCSF, 2009c).

Inclusion Development Programme – Supporting Children on the Autistic Spectrum: Guidance for Practitioners in the Early Years Foundation Stage (DCSF, 2009b).

Building Futures: Developing Trust – A Focus on Provision for Children from Gypsy, Roma and Traveller Backgrounds in the Early Years Foundation Stage (DCSF, 2009).

An inclusion resources list and information on integrated working, *Early Support* and health resources are available at: www.dcsf.gov.uk/everychildmatters/

Further information on Integrated Working, the Common Assessment Framework and the Lead Professional is available on the CWDC website at: www.cwdcouncil.org.uk/what-is-integrated-working

Further information on persona dolls is available on the persona doll website: www.persona-doll-training.org/

5 A safe and stimulating environment

CHAPTER OBJECTIVES

This chapter explores features of safe and stimulating environments in Early Years settings, and considers how these support young children's learning and development. Interpretations of the terms 'safe' and 'stimulating' are examined, and the subject of 'challenging' and 'risky' play is discussed. The provision of a safe and stimulating environment is a requirement of 'Enabling Environments', which is one of the four EYFS themes. Various aspects of this theme are considered in this chapter, including the provision of indoor, outdoor and emotional environments. Relevant EYP Standards are introduced throughout the chapter and these are explored in the context of examples from practice.

After reading this chapter you should be able to:
- consider how features of a child's learning environment support their development and individual needs;
- explore the subjects of 'challenging' and 'risky' play;
- examine ways in which you could develop and improve the environment in your setting.

Though reference is made to Standards 8, 9, 11, 12 and 19 in particular, other standards are also relevant to this chapter.

Introduction

This chapter first explores how a safe and stimulating environment supports individual children's learning and development, and considers the impact of the environment on children's well-being and self-esteem. We examine how the provision of a safe and stimulating environment contributes towards the creation of an 'Enabling Environment', one of the core EYFS themes.

You will be encouraged to reflect on the impact of current concerns about children's safety and vulnerability, and the notion that childhood is *becoming undermined by risk aversion* (Gill, 2007, p10). We will see how the provision of a challenging environment can present issues; however, if managed safely, such environments have the potential to greatly enable children's learning and development. We examine how you might address parental or practitioners' concerns about children's safety within a setting's indoor and outdoor provision through taking effective measures and also engaging in constructive dialogue with children, parents and colleagues.

We also consider how the EYFS sets out specific welfare requirements for safe practices, including the suitability of people, premises and equipment, and the need for risk assessment to cover anything with which a child may come into contact (DCSF, 2008a). An extensive list of aspects of indoor and outdoor areas requiring risk assessment is noted in Section 3 of the EYFS Practice Guidance (DCSF, 2008d). Through the use of a relevant case study, we will see that it is possible to provide a stimulating environment by managing the risks associated with a more challenging environment.

The presence of safe and stimulating environments has been found to be one of the characteristics of a continuously improving Early Years setting (DCSF, 2008d). Features of such environments, which are concerned with the need for continuous improvement, are examined in this chapter, alongside the relevant EYP Standards. For example, S12 requires EYPs to ensure resources are safe and that children know how to use them appropriately (CWDC, 2008). Resources play a key role in developing the quality and effectiveness of provision in the setting, and this chapter therefore concludes by considering how an environment benefited from the innovative use of resources by an EYP.

Safe and stimulating environments

'Staying safe' is one of the five *Every Child Matters* outcomes (DfES, 2004) that are embedded within the EYFS. To help achieve this outcome, the EYFS requires the provision of a Key Person, who should aim to meet the needs of individual children in their care (DCSF, 2008a). Whether you are a Key Person for a group of children or are supporting others in the role of Key Person, you should carefully consider how you demonstrate sensitive attitudes when responding to children. By forming close and genuine relationships with children and working collaboratively with their families, a Key Person supports the provision of an environment that is both emotionally and physically safe. Children are then able to take on new challenges, think creatively and feel confident and settled. As mentioned in the previous chapter, you will examine the role of the Key Person in more detail in Chapter 6. It can therefore be argued (DCSF, 2008i) that the provision of an emotionally safe and secure environment is a prerequisite for creating a mentally and physically challenging environment.

Children's well-being and safety is of paramount concern for all EYPs. The EYFS welfare requirements, referred to in the introduction to this chapter, provide an overarching safety framework for Early Years practice. It is important to establish a safe environment and ensure that your setting is compliant with EYFS requirements, as set out in S19 (CWDC, 2008). The following reflective task enables you to explore the features of a safe and stimulating environment.

Refer to Figure 5.1 and consider the notion of a safe and stimulating environment that:

* *promotes physical, mental and emotional health and well-being;*

* *has sufficient space for children to play and have opportunities to be outdoors with freedom to explore and be physically active;*

* *provides dynamic and flexible systems of physical organisation that support personalised learning for all children;*

* *provides continuity of care that enables children to identify with key workers and develop relationships at all levels*

Source: adapted from DCSF (2008d, p10)

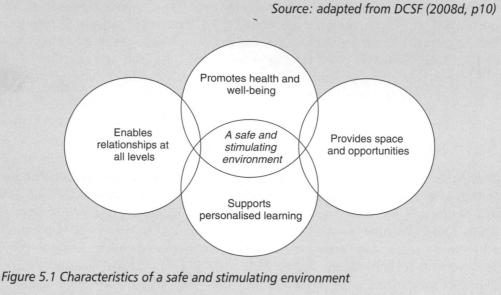

Figure 5.1 Characteristics of a safe and stimulating environment

Source: adapted from DCSF (2008d, p10)

Reflecting on Figure 5.1, now consider how you:

* *provide a 'safe and stimulating environment';*

* *lead and support others to provide a 'safe and stimulating environment'.*

It is useful to identify specific aspects of provision that support a child to feel safe and stimulated. For example, the provision of role-play activities offers a safe environment in which children can express their feelings and emotions in a meaningful context that is largely unconstrained (Siraj-Blatchford *et al.*, 2002a). Role-play opportunities should be based on themes that engage and sustain children's interest, enable them to experience different perspectives and try out alternative approaches. By joining in the role play, children can tackle more demanding tasks, which help them develop coping strategies and feel more confident.

While the EYFS Welfare Requirements (DCSF 2008a) specify procedures that aim to ensure children's safety within Early Years practice, you should also consider that notions of safe environments can be problematic. Tovey (2007) contends that conceptual understanding of terms such as 'safe' are socially constructed and are, therefore, dependent on different people's interpretations of what might constitute a 'safe' environment for children. This viewpoint has implications for S19, which states that EYPs *make sure that the environment indoors and outdoors, including furniture, equipment and toys, is safe, secure and appropriate for the children involved* (CWDC, 2008, p37). For example, there could be tensions within a team of practitioners or between practitioners and parents about whether children's use of equipment provided in the setting is deemed to be safe or unsafe. Interpretations of terms such as a 'safe environment', therefore, need to be discussed and shared by practitioners in Early Years settings so that their practice is based on greater common understanding.

Tovey (2007) suggests, too, that contemporary discourse on children's play and exploration has focused on perceived concerns about safety and risk taking. This has resulted in the expression of a prevailing negative view of risk, which has overshadowed the potential beneficial effects for children's play and exploration. However, an environment that provides little or no challenge could impede children's development of skills that enable them to be safe, and may also engender more fearful or reckless behaviours in children's future encounters with such situations. Preventing children from engaging in risk taking can, therefore, deny them opportunities to develop risk awareness, test new ideas and persist with challenges *as problems to enjoy, rather than things to fear* (Tovey, 2007, p105).

Self-assessment task

What is a safe and secure environment? Is it one where children are protected from every possible source of harm and thereby kept dependent, metaphorically wrapped in cotton wool?

(Tovey, 2007, p101)

Reflecting on the above questions, consider your response to the following.

- What are the significant risks to children's safety in the environment of your setting?

- Should children be protected from all sources of harm?

- Can we completely eliminate risk in the environment?

- Can we keep children safe if we are not constantly by their side?

Source: adapted from DCSF (2009b)

Now consider the following statements and reflect on the questions that follow them.

I believe we are taking away from children the right to learn about dangers. We need risks to discover the consequences . . . of hazards and how to take sensible risks in the future.

(Knight, 2009, p35)

Supporting children in taking risks, both physical and mental, in their play, helps them to develop vital expertise in both assessing and managing risk in everyday life, to extend their learning . . . as well as supporting their emotional well-being and resilience.

(Robson, 2010, p224)

- Why is it important that children take some risks?
- What are 'sensible' risks?
- How can we support children to take risks?
- How can practitioners involve children and their families in assessing and managing risk?

Source: adapted from DCSF (2009b)

The statements in the above task promote the potential benefits of 'risk' and 'challenge' in Early Years provision. As an EYP, you may encounter parents' fears and concerns about their children's safety, as well as practitioners' unease, or even anxiety, about the provision of 'challenging' play. There may be genuine concern expressed about the use of the indoor or outdoor environments, and sound reasons given for limiting or even denying access to certain spaces; these concerns would need to be acknowledged and sensitively addressed. However, Ouvry (2003) explains that a desire to remove all 'risky' aspects of provision could be based on uncertainties and doubts rather than real knowledge and understanding of children's interests and needs. To help you manage such attitudes, it is helpful to draw on your knowledge and understanding of children's development and policy guidance.

An EYP should consider the extent to which risk taking should be embedded into the policies and practices in your setting, and you are encouraged to draw on your knowledge of best practice in order to influence this process (S35) (CWDC, 2008). When developing or reviewing the policies in your setting, it is important that action is taken to counter any views that are not supportive of children's rights (S18). By seeking to develop environments that enable children to 'take risks and make mistakes' (S19), EYPs can demonstrate the value of *risky, skinned knee play*, which helps children take on future challenges in both the built and natural environment (Frost, 2010, p267). Discussing the perceived benefits of 'risk' and 'challenge' in children's environments with practitioners and parents also helps to bring a more balanced perspective to the debate on this subject.

PRACTICAL TASK

Consider the assumptions listed in the table below, which relate to the use of outdoor environments, and reflect on how you might respond to each of these views. Despite outdoor play being a requirement within the EYFS, children's access to the outdoor environment might be restricted by practitioners or parents who make such assumptions. This is, of course, only a theoretical exercise; in reality any concerns would need to be carefully addressed within the context in which they were expressed, and decisions about the safe use of outdoor or indoor spaces would need to be made on the basis of an actual risk assessment. Nevertheless, it is useful to consider your possible response to these

PRACTICAL TASK *continued*

assumptions, to explore the rationale on which your response is based, and to identify any relevant EYP Standards.

Assumptions about outdoor play	Your response, including the rationale upon which it is based	Relevant EYP Standards
1 The outside is dangerous		
2 Higher adult:child ratios are needed outside		
3 Educators are merely supervisors outside		
4 No learning happens outside		
5 We would go outside more if the weather was better		
6 It's more healthy to be inside than out		

Source: adapted from Ouvry (2003, pp20–25)

As an EYP, you should also have *high expectations of all children and commitment to ensuring that they can achieve their potential* (S7) (CWDC, 2008, p25). However, high expectations cannot be realised in the abstract; they require practitioners to communicate with children and their families. There needs to be an acknowledgement of children's own ability *to contribute to the situations in which they find themselves* and a genuine commitment to examine *how competent children can be* (Penn, 2008, p138). The following case study details how an EYP recognised and trusted a child's competency, which, in turn, supported the child to manage a challenging task.

CASE STUDY

Florence, an EYP in a private nursery

I recall a memorable occasion when we went on an outing. As we walked by a canal, we had to go up a stairway before reaching an open space. One child, who was just over two years old at the time, wanted to walk up the stairs unaided. I recalled that I had considered negotiating the stairs as an acceptable unaided task as part my risk assessment and so let go of the child's hand as she held onto the railing. I then stood by as the child walked all the way up the stairs by herself, shouting jubilantly 'I did it!' when she reached the top. The other children copied her and said 'I did it!', too.

Self-assessment task

Reflect on the above example from practice and answer the following questions, considering the environment of your setting.

- How well does the way you use space and resources support and extend children's all-round development during indoor and outdoor activities?

- How well do you organise the setting and overcome obstacles to provide a stimulating environment that responds to the particular needs of each child?

Source: adapted from Ofsted (2008)

Developing children's confidence and independence will also support their capacity to manage the transitions that they will encounter within and between settings. In seeking to manage these transitions when working with parents and other colleagues, an EYP will need to consider those children who may be adversely affected by transient or even incompatible arrangements of provision (S3, CWDC, 2008). This may well involve EYPs sharing information and communicating effectively with other professionals, as they seek to provide appropriate support for children during the process of transition (S36, CWDC, 2008).

Self-assessment task

Consider your understanding of:

- the transitions that young children experience as they grow and develop, and their potential effect on their learning and development (S3);

- the potential influence of particular events and situations in children's lives on their well-being, behaviour and capacity to learn (S3).

Aim to research any areas of uncertainty identified from your reflection and discuss these with your tutor or mentor. Further reading on this subject is included at the end of the chapter.

Enabling Environments

'Enabling Environments' is one of the core EYFS themes, and is expressed through the principle that the environment plays a key role in supporting and extending children's learning needs and development (DCSF, 2008e). You will support the implementation of this principle by embracing its four commitments:

3.1 Observation, assessment and planning;

3.2 Supporting every child;

3.3 The learning environment;

3.4 The wider context.

Commitment 3.2 states that *the environment supports every child's learning through planned experiences that are challenging but achievable*, while Commitment 3.3 declares that *a rich and varied environment can give children confidence to explore and learn in secure and safe, yet challenging, indoor and outdoor spaces* (DCSF, 2008e). The use of the term *challenging but achievable* in Commitment 3.2 builds upon the conclusions of the Plowden Report (DES, 1967, p196), which advised about the provision of *an environment and opportunities which are sufficiently challenging for children and yet not so difficult as to be outside of their reach*. This influential report on primary education is still pertinent today; its emphasis on play as a means of learning is embodied in the EYFS and its recommendation for a stimulating environment is expressed within S8 (CWDC, 2008). This Standard advocates the provision of a *welcoming, purposeful, stimulating and encouraging environment where children feel confident and secure and are able to develop and learn* (CWDC, 2008, p26). Therefore, it provides a basis for examining how an environment helps to motivate children's interests, is supportive of their needs and promotes their independence.

S8 also encourages EYPs to consider the quality of an enabling environment and its capacity to affect individuals, drawing on the Reggio Emilia approach, which emphasises the significance of multi-sensory environments that, for example, encourage children to look at shades of colours and consider smells and textures (Valentine, 2006). Practitioners could, therefore, consider how the environment in their setting 'speaks' to children and their families, and how it offers the potential for children to *learn from it, as well as within it and about it, and about themselves* (DCSF, 2009c, p24).

REFLECTIVE TASK

Consider the spaces, arrangement of objects, colours, textures, sights, sounds and smells in your setting, and reflect on:

- *how these contribute to the way children and adults feel, react, interact, communicate and learn in your setting;*

- *how you could develop sensory experiences for children in your setting.*

Source: adapted from DCSF (2009c)

When exploring the sensory environment in your setting, you should consider those children who may be more sensitive than others. For example, some children on the autistic spectrum could be over-sensitive (hypersensitive) to certain stimuli, while others may be under-sensitive, which could engender self-harming behaviours (DCSF, 2009b). Advice from other professionals could assist you not only in meeting individual children's needs but to support your consideration about the affective quality of the environment. Developing or fostering effective relationships with parents, and encouraging them to share information about their children of a more sensitive or confidential nature would also support your provision of an enabling environment that meets the specific needs of individual children more effectively (S30, CWDC, 2008).

Providing an enabling environment is also incorporated into S11, which is concerned with safeguarding children's welfare *without restricting their opportunities to develop* (CWDC, 2008, p29). The following task encourages you to explore the characteristics of the provision in your setting within the context of S11.

Self-assessment task

S11 is concerned with experiences that EYPs provide in different contexts, which enable young children to develop and learn. Key characteristics of these experiences are described in the following list:

- *planned and purposeful*, giving all children opportunities to learn and develop;
- *relevant*, with content that matches children's ages, needs, interests and learning styles;
- *developmentally appropriate* for children's different starting points from which they develop their learning;
- *sustained* so they give children time to become engrossed, to work in depth and to complete activities;
- *comprehensive* in that they cover all aspects of the EYFS.

Source: adapted from CWDC (2008)

As you reflect on the list above, think of an example from practice in your setting for each of these characteristics and note these in the table below. You may have more than one example for each key characteristic and you should also add any possible sources of evidence to demonstrate how you are meeting S11, as well as other relevant EYP Standards.

Key characteristics of experiences provided that enable young children to develop and learn	Examples from your practice	Possible sources of evidence and relevant EYP Standards
Planned and purposeful		
Relevant		
Developmentally appropriate		
Sustained		
Comprehensive		

The learning environment

As described in the EYFS, the learning environment consists of the indoor, outdoor and emotional environments (DCSF, 2008e). The provision of effective learning environments for children's play and exploration should be contended as part of any conception of Early Years practice (Siraj-Blatchford *et al.*, 2002a). The following case study illustrates how an EYP and Children's Centre manager developed provision of stimulating indoor, outdoor and emotional environments for families who attended her setting. Looking at each 'environment' separately supports a more focused consideration of their unique qualities. However, each 'environment' should not be seen as a separate entity within the overall provision of children's learning and development, as there is a clear interrelationship between these three environments.

CASE STUDY

Fiona, an EYP and Children's Centre manager

Development of an enabling environment: indoors

The most obvious development would be through having accessible resources that are clearly labelled with photos, Makaton* symbols and language. Labelling everything not only supports children to access toys and equipment independently but also aids in the tidying-up process.

Development of an enabling environment: outdoors

The outdoor space has taken a longer period of time to evolve but has been definitely worth it as it gains the most praise from our families. As the setting is located in an area of London where few people have gardens or access to green space, we decided to make the outdoor area as wild and real as possible. There are no static climbing frames or plastic, primary-coloured slides. Instead, we have willow arbours, bushes for den building, a vegetable patch, wildlife area and a hobbit house. The outdoor space is real, natural and much freer for imaginative play than prescriptive equipment.

Development of an enabling environment: the emotional environment

As children stay within the setting for up to ten hours a day, I set about ensuring that the ending of the day was as homely as possible. There is still access to play resources should children wish to use these, but there are also fluffy sofas and blankets, a TV in a corner of the room and a dining table with adult chairs where the children eat their tea. In this way we hope that we are replicating the environment at home, and since introducing the new cosy 'home' room, we have observed an increase in settling of children.

* Makaton is a system of communication that involves signs and speech to support a child's understanding (see 'Further reading' at the end of Chapter 4).

Referring to Fiona's account of the development of each environment in the case study above, consider a response to the following questions.

Question	Your response	EYP Standards that are relevant to this example of provision
How does Fiona provide activities that are based on a clear rationale?		
How does Fiona foster children's independence?		
How does Fiona promote children's personal, social and emotional development?		
How does Fiona build upon children's own initiatives and choices?		
How does the provision in one environment (indoor, outdoor or emotional) impact upon another?		

Source: adapted from CWDC (2008)

The above case study reveals how an EYP can facilitate children's learning and development by encouraging them to create their own places to play. In this example, the EYP's development of the emotional environment also supported the children to be more inclined to access the provision available both indoors and outdoors.

As an EYP, you will be required to *listen to parents with due respect* (S29, CWDC, 2008, p56) and to maintain *positive and effective relationships and communication with parents* (S30, CWDC, 2008, p57). Evidence from research demonstrates that the outcome of collaboration between parents and practitioners has a positive impact on children's learning and development (DCSF, 2008d). These relationships are also a key component within the environment of the Reggio Emilia approach, as they provide children with a *sense of security that derives from feeling welcome and valued at the same time* (Rinaldi, 2006, p84).

Another aspect of Reggio Emilia practice is the process of ongoing assessment, which is known as 'documentation'. Through this system, dialogue occurs between educators and children about their interests, ideas and work. Their thinking and activity is recorded and reviewed on a regular basis, and a record of photographs, drawings and conversations is compiled, which is accessible to children, staff and parents. The value of this record lies not just in the information it contains but the wider message it exudes. Documentation openly declares that learning is both valuable and valued, and is a thoughtful, reflective and extensive process that is respectful of children's agency to make contributions to their own learning and development. Moreover, assessment of their learning is derived not only from adult constructs of worthwhile evidence but can rely on different forms of data that are created with the active participation of the learner. We explore in more detail the underpinning philosophy and pedagogy of Reggio Emilia in Chapter 9.

PRACTICAL TASK

Consider how children share or celebrate their efforts and achievements with others in your setting, either individually or as a participant in group learning contexts. Then respond to the following questions.

- *Can children choose examples of their work that they feel are worthy to share or display?*

- *Are display boards presented at children's height, so they can share some responsibility about work displayed?*

- *Are there meaningful contexts to encourage reciprocal communication between adults and children about their learning?*

- *Can children refer to their previous work so that they can use it as a springboard for their next steps?*

Source: adapted from Brooker (2008, p131) and DCSF (2008j, p15)

Now draw a map of your setting based on your responses to the above questions about the learning environment in your setting. Your map should illustrate all the opportunities that are available for children to document their efforts and achievements. Then consider if these opportunities are consistently applied and valued in your setting. Identify any areas for future action and highlight these on your map.

You should also consider how forms of new technology can contribute to the process of documenting children's learning – for example, children's own use of digital photography, which can document a sequential process over time. Digital photographs can also readily be shared with parents in compliance with any digital image policy within the setting. An EYP will need to ensure that suitable measures are in place to protect images of children held by the setting, as well as other safety aspects relating to the use of technology. For example, EYPs should review children's safe access and use of ICT equipment, and help them to develop their awareness of potential health risks from using computers and other electronic equipment.

Children have had far greater opportunity in recent years to access the internet and they will need guidance to use this technology safely. Parents may have concerns about their children's use of such technology, so clear communication on the setting's policy and safeguards will help to allay their fears (S19) (CWDC, 2008). EYPs should also consider both positive and negative aspects about the use of technology and not be swayed by more dominant concerns about the dangers of the use of technology. The Byron Review (DCSF, 2008k) considered the issue of inappropriate material that is available on the internet, and provided recommendations on how to keep children and young people safe in digital environments; these recommendations can support the development and review of policy that aims to keep young children safe online (DCSF, 2009d).

Developing the environment

The final section of this chapter encourages you to consider the development of the environment in your setting. This will be based on your ongoing evaluation of the existing provision, careful observations of children's interaction within their environment, and consideration of the views of children, their parents and other practitioners who use the setting. It is also useful here to draw upon EYFS guidance regarding the development of different aspects of the learning environment (DCSF, 2008d).

REFLECTIVE TASK

Review the guidance below on the provision for children's learning and development, which has been categorised into three sections. You may find it helpful to first consider environmental factors within your own childhood experiences, which you feel have affected your learning and development, before exploring the practice in your setting. As you consider each section of the task, you are encouraged to review these areas against the practice in your setting. Consider, too, what action you might take to implement change and enhance areas of the environment to promote children's learning and development:

Part 1

Reflecting on the environment in your setting, consider whether the provision for children's learning and development presents:

* *some materials and resources familiar to the children from their home and community environments;*

* *materials that have many uses, such as wooden hoops and pegs in a tin, with unlimited opportunities for children to use them creatively and imaginatively to support their learning and development;*

* *surfaces and levels, places to sit or lie, to climb or swing, and to make big movements such as spinning, dancing, jumping, running and so on.*

Part 2

Now reflect on opportunities that children in your setting have to:

* *dig, climb, swing, move, stretch and crawl, and to control wheeled toys;*

- *touch and feel a variety of textures, make marks, cut and join materials together, or shape and construct materials;*

- *rest and refresh themselves;*

- *have time to play with what interests them and make choices;*

- *watch the natural world changing, to explore and solve problems;*

- *make friends and develop relationships;*

- *learn and develop at their own pace.*

Part 3

Finally, consider if practitioners in your setting:

- *offer a range of experiences and resources that are regularly monitored and refreshed to keep them safe and stimulating;*

- *tune in to the children's interests and interact with them to support and extend their learning and development, jointly engaging in problem solving and sustained shared thinking;*

- *respond to observed interests, and plan new materials and experiences within the environment that reflect these;*

- *provide materials that reflect diversity in order to avoid stereotypical images or approaches;*

- *evaluate their provision to ensure that everything that is provided is of the highest quality;*

- *consult and engage families in choosing the materials and resources the children use in the setting so that links can be made with the home;*

- *support children's confidence in themselves and their developing skills as they tackle new experiences and develop a sense of what they can do and what they will be able to do as they practise and meet the challenges in the environment.*

Source: adapted from 'Effective practice: the learning environment', in DCSF (2008d)

Another aspect of provision is described in the following case study, which provides an account of how an EYP developed heuristic play (Goldschmied and Jackson, 2004) for babies, which was then embedded into the daily routine of the baby room. This example of practice is particularly relevant to S9, but it also relates to other EYP Standards and you are encouraged to identify these as you reflect on this case study.

Tanya, an EYP in a Children's Centre

A specific interaction with a child with autism, who was comforted with fascination and calm, after an angry and physical outburst, by my muslin scarf led me to think about the range of quality provision relating to senses. I wanted to extend the opportunity for heuristic play and provide a range of interesting resources for babies, to promote their curiosity and independence. Much deliberation and conflicts of interest had occurred over where and when heuristic sessions could take place. This had been the main reason for the heuristic play sessions not occurring previously. I identified an urgent need to find a dedicated time and place to ensure implementation as these restrictions had put questions over the operational usage of the resources. I audited each area in terms of strengths and weaknesses in relation to time and space, as well as the guidance provided. Having completed the audit, a large space within the baby nest room was dedicated to heuristic play sessions and large mats were ordered. The mats arrived and the staff were delighted.

All the materials for heuristic play were sorted and rearranged, and organised into 14 draw-string bags. These were then located on a peg rack in the baby room at eye level for children, and labelled with photographs. Matching bag labels were added to encourage children's autonomy in learning. I was delighted when one baby was immediately drawn to the photograph of the wooden rings. He was seemingly mesmerised and saying 'circle' – providing further evidence of his interesting dynamic circular schema. He then became particularly attached to the rings and would carry one in each hand, and he was able to add to the resources to develop his interests.

After reflecting on observations of the children, I began refining the quality and range of provision to explore skills and develop interests. This resulted in investigations by children into collecting, sorting, building, filling and emptying; both refining fine motor control skills and encouraging independence and creative thinking. Progress in terms of the EYFS and areas of learning and development was encouraging. I made a display and added photographs of children engaged in heuristic play above the peg bags, and added quotes and statements about heuristic play to develop understanding for parents, visitors and other practitioners. Particularly successful heuristic play sessions occurred when the objects reflected and extended children's interests. The objects were combined at times with other media such as scarves or lightweight colourful balls, which I added to develop tactile experiences.

Wonderful interaction occurred between the children, myself and other adults, including good eye contact, encouragement, occasional parallel play and the giving of support when needed, including imitation and mirroring. The skill levels of babies fascinated me and were observed through narrative and through photographs – with precise hand control, even sculptures were created. At the end of the sessions I encouraged many babies to be actively engaged with putting resources away. The children responded well to participating in clearing away the resources, and were autonomous and independent in carrying the bags and looking after the resources. Reviewing resources and extending provision is a continuous process, and it is important to actively engage and involve others in this process.

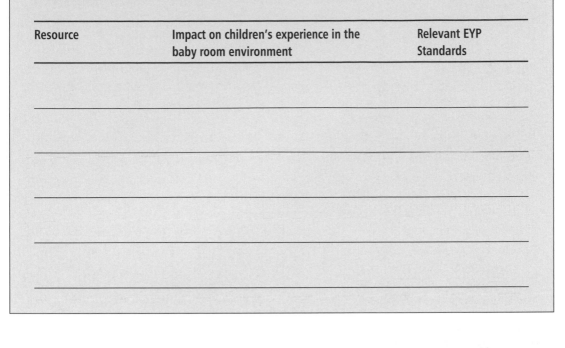

PRACTICAL TASK

In the table below, list some of the specific resources that Tanya introduced into the environment of the baby room to support the development of heuristic play. Next to each of these resources, describe their impact on children's experience of play. You are encouraged to note any relevant EYP Standards.

Resource	Impact on children's experience in the baby room environment	Relevant EYP Standards

C H A P T E R   S U M M A R Y

This chapter has focused on the provision of a safe and stimulating environment that supports young children's learning and development. We have explored the concept of the enabling environment, which is premised upon the provision of an effective learning environment that supports children's development and well-being. Relevant EYP Standards have been explored regarding secure, safe – yet challenging – provision within the environment. We have also discussed how collaborative working with parents and other practitioners can lead to shared understandings of more challenging experiences that promote children's confidence and independence. EYPs should undertake a process of regular review and evaluation of the learning environment to ensure safe practices are maintained and to identify areas for development.

Moving on

In developing a more enabling environment, EYPs must foster enhanced relationships to support effective interactions with children; this aspect of practice is explored in greater depth in the following chapter.

FURTHER READING

DCSF (2008i) *Social and Emotional Aspects of Development: Guidance for Practitioners Working in the Early Years Foundation Stage*. Nottingham: DCSF.

DfES (2006) *Seamless Transitions – Supporting Continuity in Young Children's Learning*. Available online at: www.teachernet.gov.uk/publications.

Tovey, H (2007) *Playing Outdoors: Spaces and Places, Risks and Challenge*. Maidenhead: OUP.

6 The role of the EYP in supporting children's learning

CHAPTER OBJECTIVES

This chapter explores in more depth aspects of the EYP role – the pedagogue role – in supporting young children to learn effectively. The concept of the Key Person is examined, and Bruner's concept of scaffolding and Pascal and Bertram's work on adult involvement in children's learning form a focus for the discussion. The levels and quality of interaction between practitioner and child, especially in play situations, are considered. A range of case studies, reflective tasks and practical activities are offered to support your developing understanding of this aspect of Early Years pedagogy and the application of this to your own role.

After reading this chapter you should be able to:
- critically appraise the concept of the 'Key Person' role – and how critical this is to effective practice;
- identify the strengths of the integrated pedagogical model, which balances adult-led/adult-initiated activities with those that are child led/child initiated;
- evaluate the adult's role in scaffolding children's learning (Bruner, 1978);
- discuss the three core elements of effective adult–child interactions, especially in play activities, as identified by Pascal and Bertram (2001), based on Ferre Laevers' (1994) Scale of Adult Engagement Scale;
- begin to apply these insights into your own role and practice.

In this chapter, there is a focus on very many of the Standards and, in particular, on S11, 12, 13, 14, 15, 17, 18, 19, 20, 21, 22, 23, 24, 25, 26, 27 and 28.

Introduction

'High expectations of all children . . .'

. . . thus reads Early Years Professional Status (EYPS) Standard 7 (CWDC, 2008, p25), which is the first of the 18 Standards that form the group classed as 'Effective Practice'. Standard 24, the final one in this group, requires the EYP to be *accountable for the delivery of high quality provision* (CWDC, 2008, p43). Acting rather as 'bookends' for this group of Standards, then – with each of them emphasising the 'raising' of the quality of Early Years provision – there is opportunity to focus very specifically here on your own understanding of what constitutes 'high' expectations and effective provision. Given the emphasis on the EYP role in leading practice, such understanding must essentially be modelled in your own relationships and interactions with children. This can be demonstrated specifically through a successful key person system, through your understanding of the practitioner role in supporting learning and development, and in the quality of the interpersonal relationships and interactions between practitioner and child.

The Key Person role

The importance of the Key Person (KP) role and the need that young children have for secure attachments were noted in Chapters 4 and 5. The significance of its inclusion in the Statutory Framework of the EYFS (DCSF, 2008a) was summarised effectively by Evans (2008), who described Key Persons as the *lynchpins* of any Early Years setting. Research (see, for example, Trevarthen, 2001; David *et al.*, 2003; Elfer *et al.*, 2003) suggests that the Key Person is a particularly crucial role for children under three, and the seminal work of Goldschmied and Jackson (2004) established understanding of its importance for our youngest children. The approach was initially described as 'care assignment' with the intention of addressing the experience of 'multiple indiscriminate care', which was observed in day care provision during the 1980s (Bain and Barnett, 1986). Increasingly, we have come to learn that children learn to be strong and independent from a base of loving and secure relationships with parents and/or a substitute 'Key Person' (DCSF, 2008e, 2.4). There is less research evidence to date of the benefits of the system for older children within the EYFS but, arguably, this continues to allow staff to develop a deeper knowledge of individual children, to focus specifically on them and their needs, and to work in close and meaningful partnership with their families.

As an EYP, you may well fulfil the KP role yourself; equally, you may have lead responsibility for the effective implementation of the KP system. Either way, successful delivery of the EYFS will depend to a large extent on how effective a setting's KP system is. When it works well, a Key Person system ensures that the benefits of the approach include:

- a genuine bond is established between the Key Person, the individual child and her/his family;
- a settled, close relationship is forged;
- children feel safe and cared for;
- parents are reassured that their child is being responded to sensitively and with care.

REFLECTIVE TASK

Read the following accounts of how EYPs' experience the KP systems in their settings, and then answer the questions that follow.

CASE STUDY

Menna, EYP and manager of a pre-school offering sessional care

I have introduced a Key Person system in my setting. We operate in one room with children aged from two to four years. My aim was to introduce a high-quality functional KP system drawn from a genuine desire to get to know each child and their carers and families. I attended a recent course led by Marion Dowling, who described practitioners as 'companions in children's play' and I feel this describes both my understanding of the core KP role and my intention for the setting. I led a staff training session on the KP system and my staff now recognise that unless children have built healthy secondary attachments they are unlikely to be able to engage in their play in such a way that leads to 'deep learning'.

CASE STUDY

Judith, manager of a pre-school playgroup and currently on the long pathway to EYPS

At first, for a range of complex reasons, my staff were very reluctant to participate in a KP system in the setting, but the introduction of the EYFS provided me with the opportunity to develop the system and it was great to see the whole team gradually seeing the importance of this in supporting both the child and the child's family. By working closely with the child and family, the KP has been able to gain valuable information that is used to ensure the child feels safe and secure and that our learning environment is meeting the needs of the child.

CASE STUDY

Pam, EYP and a childminder

While other types of setting are still coming to terms with this aspect of the Statutory Framework of the EYFS, to childminders this type of approach is very familiar because we are the child's main – usually the only – carer within the setting. I quickly establish a strong emotional bond with all the children in my care and children quickly feel at home within my setting. The two and a half year old I look after at the moment refers to me as 'My Pam' when talking to his family and other people!

CASE STUDY

Sandra, EYP and manager of a private nursery

I believe the KP system, combined with our practice of home visits, has contributed significantly to the quality and equality of practice in my setting. These allow for the development of a very close partnership between families and setting. I have a group of key children, as do all our staff, and as a KP, I believe we uphold children's rights, and take responsibility for each feeling valued and included. And because we have close relationships with families, it is easier for them to discuss their needs with us and, therefore, to have their needs met. Children and parents feel that they know their KP well and these relationships continue to grow and develop over time.

REFLECTIVE TASK

- *How are each of these EYPs demonstrating effective personal practice and/or leadership of others in the way they are implementing the KP system in their settings?*
- *What is your experience to date of this system?*
- *What are the challenges in effective implementation of the KP system?*

Challenges of the Key Person system

No doubt, having reflected on the third question above, you have identified a number of challenges in the implementation of the KP approach in practice. Issues such as teamwork and establishing a collaborative approach to practice have been addressed previously by the authors in discourse exploring the leadership aspects of the EYP role (Whalley *et al.*, 2008). One theme shared by Menna and Judith above is the importance of staff training in order that each KP has a sound grasp of the importance of the role. In essence, the KP has a three-fold responsibility: to the child, the family and the setting. Evans (2008) describes the effective KP as:

- committed to the role;
- a good communicator;
- calm and confident;
- open and sensitive, especially during the settling-in process;
- discreet – never forgetting that parents are a child's first 'Key Person';
- able to form healthy attachments;
- able to provide appropriate comfort and reassurance;
- able to gather and share relevant information;
- able to prioritise time in order to communicate regularly and effectively with parents.

Few would question such characteristics of effectiveness; yet the gap between rhetoric and reality can be huge, and the skilled EYP needs to be secure in their own understanding of the pedagogical principles that underpin the KP role, and committed to the quality training of staff for whom they have leadership responsibilities. The EYP may also have line management responsibilities for a setting's KPs and as such needs to take responsibility for:

- induction systems into the setting's KP system for new staff;

- organising an effective welcome and settling-in process for all children;

- organising a 'cover' system for when the named KP is absent, and devising a system for sharing information between colleagues at 'handover' times;

- organising a supportive transition system as children move within and beyond the setting.

Source: adapted from Evans (2008, p29)

Such issues relate to a setting's organisation and management, and need careful thought and planning. Less easy to manage is the *painfulness of children's preferences* (Elfer, 2009, p11). One of the challenges of the KP role can be the lack of meaningful bonding between a child and the KP. A KP does need to be able to offer the *consistent emotional support and care* (Grenier, 2005) that young children need. Experience suggests that – for a range of complex reasons – some adults fail to connect at an emotional level with certain children – and vice versa – and, increasingly, settings are adopting the approach taken at Becky's setting, as described in the case study that follows.

CASE STUDY

Becky, at the point of EYPS validation and assistant manager at a Children's Centre

As a setting, we implemented the KP system long before it became a statutory requirement and used to pre-allocate a KP to our children before they started. We no longer do this, but rather when children attend the centre for their pre-setting visits, we note which of the practitioners they make bonds with and it is from this that a KP is identified.

REFLECTIVE TASK

- *What are the advantages of the kind of self-selection approach described in the above case study? How might such an approach be justified from a pedagogical base?*

- *What might be the challenges of this approach in your setting and how could you overcome these?*

The EYP as enabler and facilitator of children's learning

Siraj-Blatchford *et al.* (2002a, p10) argue that *if learning comes from a process of cognitive construction that is only achieved when the child is motivated and involved . . . [then] . . . it is entirely consistent to treat the part played by the effective educator the same way*. The essential roles of such an effective practitioner have been identified as those of observer, enabler and facilitator (Moyles *et al.*, 2002a). Skills in observation have been identified in a useful resource in this series of publications (Palaiologou, 2008). Here we turn to those other concepts: enabling and facilitating learning. From our consideration of theoretical influences on Early Years pedagogy, we know that children learn best through their interactions with people who know and relate to them well (Bandura, 1977; Rogoff, 1990). Bruner's (1978) concept of 'scaffolding' is central to the understanding of the EYP's personal practice and in modelling this to colleagues. For learning to take place, effective social interactional frameworks need to be in place in which the adult has progressively higher expectations of the child's – specifically linguistic – contribution. Bruner argues that it is within such a 'scaffold' that language is acquired and used meaningfully. The adult can scaffold the child's learning in a planned instructional situation (Applebee and Langer, 1983), such as in a planned small-group activity introducing new artefacts or concepts. Equally, Long and Sato (1984) see the importance of 'conversational scaffolding' such as those interactions that take place spontaneously in routine activities, for instance, at meal and snack times. Look at how two EYPs describe their understanding and experience of scaffolding.

CASE STUDY

Menna, EYP and manager of a pre-school offering sessional care

I use my knowledge and understanding of child development to scaffold children's play, covering all the areas of learning, noting significant steps and identifying appropriate resources and activities for their 'next steps'. I ensure that my staff understand this key aspect of their role and can respond appropriately to children, offering them extension resources to promote and develop their interests and so enhance their learning. For me, scaffolding is essentially about facilitating those 'next steps' for each child.

CASE STUDY

Jack, EYP and pre-school leader at a Children's Centre

I like to picture scaffolding as 'enabling children to get further up the building' of learning and development through the way I support them in activities. Sometimes, I will sit and plan how I will do this beforehand. For instance, two of our children were expressing a particular interest in hairdressing. With colleagues, I decided to introduce a basketful of 'hairdressing resources' to the children in a group activity (later developed into role play) –

CASE STUDY *continued*

to introduce them to new vocabulary and enable them to reflect and share on their experiences of haircuts etc. Equally, I try to use every opportunity to enhance the children's knowledge and understanding. Recently, when I was cleaning up a child's knee after she fell in the outdoor area, we got into a deep conversation about cats. This was completely out of the blue – but I think we both learned a lot through our chat. For me 'scaffolding' and 'sustained shared learning' are flip sides of the same coin.

REFLECTIVE TASK

- *What links can you make between Menna's experience in the case study above and Standard 14?*

- *Can you think of examples from your own experience – as Jack does in the case study – of both planned and unplanned 'scaffolding'? What links do you make, as Jack does here, with Standard 16?*

Children's learning and 'teacher' style: the work of Ferre Laevers

The work of Ferre Laevers at Leuven University in Belgium is now acknowledged worldwide (Stephen, 2006). Based on Laevers' observations of young children, and his belief that they regularly become 'lost' in what they are doing, this focus on young children's absorption in learning (Laevers, 1994) has been widely welcomed in Early Years practice globally. Laevers *et al.* (2005, p10) are convinced that involved children are gaining a deep, motivated, intense and long-term learning experience, *at the very limit of their capabilities*. In expounding the model of Experiential Education (EXE), Laevers (2003) highlights an inextricable link between such 'deep learning' and children's well-being and urges that, rather than look at *outcomes* of learning, we should – rather – focus on processes and achievements *in* learning. The Leuven Involvement Scale (Laevers, 1994) provides a consistent method by which this can be measured. It is a tool for use by practitioners to observe a list of signals indicating learning that can be recorded on a five-point scale, ranging from Level 1, where a *child may seem absent and display no energy; the activity is simple repetitive and passive*, to Level 5 where *the child is fully concentrated, creative, energetic and persistent, with intense activity revealing the greatest involvement* (Laevers et al., 2005, p14).

Research with the Leuven Involvement Scale (Laevers, 1994) has shown that the levels of involvement within a setting tend to be more or less stable. Laevers (2006, p6) describes such involvement as *the result of the interactions between the context (including the way 'teachers' handle their group) and the characteristics of the children themselves*, and suggests that the more competent the teacher, the higher the level of the child's involvement can be. The large-scale Effective Early Learning (EEL) project in the UK (Pascal and Bertram, 2001; Pascal *et al.*, 1998), involving more than 5,000 adults using the Leuven Involvement Scale to observe more than 50,000 pre-school children, provides further helpful insights on the impact of 'teacher style' on children's learning and well-being. For our purposes, the term 'teacher' includes all adults who are involved in supporting teaching and learning in young children. The EEL project identifies three core elements in an adult's style that can shape early learning: levels of sensitivity; the amount of stimulation; and the 'allowing' of autonomy.

1. *Sensitivity* – where the adult demonstrates sensitivity to the feelings and emotional well-being of the child, and includes elements of sincerity, empathy, responsiveness and affection.

2. *Stimulation* – the way the adult intervenes in a learning process and the content of such interventions.

3. *Autonomy* – the degree of freedom the adult gives the child to experiment, make judgements, choose activities and express ideas.

Source: adapted from Pascal and Bertram (2001)

REFLECTIVE TASK

Look again at Standards 11, 14, 22, 23 and 27. Think about how the above concepts of 'sensitivity', 'stimulation' and 'autonomy' link to these. Can you think of examples from your own work setting where you have put one or other of these into practice?

Types of adult–child interactions

The concept of 'stimulation' is a highly pertinent one, not only relating to the *way* an adult intervenes in children's learning but also *when*. A number of terms are in frequent use concerning the type of interactions that are taking place when adults and children are learning together: *child initiated, child led, adult supported, adult initiated, adult-led*, and so on. You might like to stop and think about your current understanding of such terms and how you view them in the context of effective practice. For clarity, examples support the definitions listed in Table 6.1.

Critical questions for the EYP lie in knowing when it is appropriate to use each, especially when children are engaged in purposeful play – as in the examples above.

Table 6.1 Types of adult–child interactions

Child initiated	Where the child spontaneously initiates a learning situation, based on what s/he's interested in	(Example) James picks up a hammer from the tool kit and says *I'm Bob the Builder and I'm going to fix the wall*, proceeding to hammer (gently!) at the wall in the setting's indoor base room
Child led	Where the child continues to take a lead role in the learning	James may then decide to 'write out a bill' to his 'customer' for his work, find another wall that needs 'fixing' or another 'building task', invite a 'mate' (child or adult) to support his work, etc. James is in lead control of the play the whole time
Adult supported	Where the adult supports the child's idea(s) by responding to and reciprocating with her/him – optimally in response to a request for support from the child for additional resources or adaptations; though can also be effectively offered through skilful, gentle intervention in order to extend the child's learning	In the above play scenario, the practitioner might gently assume the role of James' 'customer' or 'co-worker', or invite another child to take on these roles, thus introducing a social dimension to the play as well as extending its possibilities
Adult initiated	Where the adult introduces an idea or resource to the children, possibly offering instructions or modelling its possibilities	In the light of James' play, the role-play area might be changed to become a 'builders' yard' and one or more practitioners 'model' to the children some of the play opportunities in it; the children then develop the opportunities in their own way (though may then receive adult support)
Adult led	Where the adult takes and maintains a lead in the learning situation with an express purpose in terms of introducing specific ideas and language, etc.	For instance, by setting up an outdoor obstacle course, which the practitioner introduces, models and then supervises to maximise the learning and ensure the children's safety

Look at the examples in the table below, from the practice of a range of EYPs, and make a judgement about the type(s) of interactional learning in each. You might also like to make a judgement about whether this is a 'play' or 'non-play' opportunity for learning and development.

Learning scenario	Type(s) of interactional learning	Play (P) or non-play (N-P)?
Errol, leader of the toddler room in a large private setting, is particularly passionate about the outdoors and operates a free-flow system between indoor and outdoor provision. He observes Alysha, two and a half, one of his key group, regularly going alone to different points of the perimeter of the outdoor area and – not using any resources – bending down and appearing to pick things up and put them in an imaginary container. After observing this for a few days, Errol decides – before the children arrive – to set out some natural materials (pine cones, small pebbles, etc.) and some tins and baskets around the perimeter of the area. The first time Alysha sees these she appears a little non-plussed and goes back inside but, after a few minutes, she ventures out again and makes her way to an area where Errol has set out some large twigs and baskets, and begins to arrange the twigs in a basket. Kyler joins Alysha and together they go round the whole area and put the various materials in the different containers that Errol has set out.		
Judith, leader of a pre-school, identifies that one of her key children, Salim, aged three, has a particular interest in construction, especially on 'real building sites'. She has already set up a trip for the children to the local fire station so, in planning the route, Judith makes sure the children pass the building site where a new supermarket is being constructed. As soon as they approach the site, Salim begins to count and label the number of trucks, diggers and tippers on the site, and other children join in excitedly, looking at the signs, discussing what the workers are doing, the materials being used, and identifying aspects of safety etc.		
Clare, a Children's Centre teacher and early learning consultant, makes a point of allocating an hour each week to work with one particular group of children, aged three to four, in the Centre. In her understanding of 'leader of practice', Clare is seeking to 'take staff with her' by modelling effective practice – rather than imposing change. She takes this opportunity of working with the children for storytelling and includes other staff in a support role for this. In the		

storytelling, Clare uses a range of strategies to encourage the children's involvement: asking open-ended questions to check understanding, allowing for prediction of 'What do you think happens next?' and introducing props through which the children can act out the stories.

Nancy, a childminder, has a baby, ten months, in her charge who is on the 'At Risk' register and is very fearful of loud noises or shouting by the other children. At first the child needs almost constant close physical contact with Nancy as he lacks confidence to play either on his own or with the other children. Gradually, he is observing the other children with much greater concentration and so Nancy takes the opportunity to set him at floor level, with herself positioned behind him, and they explore a stacking-type activity. Soon the baby is engrossed, though he keeps looking to Nancy for reassurance.

You should be able to see here that play is not the only way the children learn and that a variety of modes of interaction can be appropriate.

An integrated pedagogical model

There are no simple answers to such questions about adult involvement in children's learning. Increasingly, we are coming to see that effective practice includes a balance of all these modes of interactional learning (Siraj-Blatchford and Sylva, 2004). One helpful model, offered by Wood (2008) (see Figure 6.1) is that of an *integrated pedagogical model*, which confirms this balanced approach. For the EYP, this model suggests that the role is not simply about *leading play*, however central to the role this is, but also about providing for those other aspects of early learning that are so essential to effective pedagogy. These include: opportunities to learn about books through stories and rhymes; mark making and representational drawings and art work; sharing experiences and feelings through circle time; and first-hand experiences – for instance, through visits and visitors, active exploration of materials and living things.

Despite the complexity of the level, nature and timing of adult involvement in children's learning, it is an aspect of practice that is an essential element of the EYP role. The integrated pedagogical model (Wood, 2008) shows that it is the *range* of interactions that makes the whole. Arguably, the EEL project (Pascal and Bertram, 2001) both identifies the factors of quality in such interactions (characterised by sensitivity, stimulation and autonomy) and also offers important clues about the 'when to?' of adult involvement. It is very easy to misjudge – to intervene and take over a child's learning inappropriately or to miss opportunities to extend the learning through effective and timely intervention. Where adults are sensitive to the needs of the children and are 'in tune' with and responsive to

Figure 6.1 Integrated pedagogical model

Source: adapted from Wood (2008)

these, they will be mindful of the learning process that is going on and know – from both a knowledgeable, informed base *and* intuitively – when to allow the child full autonomy to explore, make judgements and make mistakes, and when and how to intervene and further scaffold the child's learning effectively. As reflective practitioners, EYPs will use the opportunity to monitor their involvement in children's learning and the way they model this to others.

Key issues in developing an integrated pedagogical approach link effectively to the EYP Standards and include:

- knowing each child well through an effective Key Person system and from a base of strong knowledge of child development (S2, 13);

- organising provision to ensure breadth, balance and inclusion (S9, 11, 12, 18);

- maximising effective use of play and talk to support learning (S11, 26, 27);

- planning for continuity, as well as balance, between adult-led and child-initiated activities (S11);

- providing progression opportunities for children's developing skills as 'players' and 'learners' (S10, 14, 21);

- allowing sufficient time for play to develop in complexity and challenge (S11).

In the following case studies, three EYPs describe their understanding of such an integrated pedagogical approach.

Pam, EYP and a childminder

I believe I offer a broad and varied programme to the children I care for. There is a lot of free play and I also encourage numeracy as part of my provision, but in an informal and fun way. The children I have at the moment have a favourite counting book called Ten Little Ladybirds, which they choose regularly. The children like to count the ladybirds with me and use their fingers to touch them as they count. This helps them to understand numbers rather than simply reciting number words. The children also like to look for numbers on houses, buses, car number plates, etc. One of my children, a little girl aged two and a half, is just gaining confidence in meaningful speech and, in play, I listen to her carefully, repeat what she has said, offering additional information and encouragement to extend her learning. I modelled this recently to a student who was on placement with me, when the child was busy brushing a doll's hair and giving it a drink. Childminding provides great opportunity to use the outdoor environment. We visit parks, shops, go to the local parent and toddler group and visit another childminder's home for play sessions. We also go further afield to visit garden centres, the woods and other places of interest. I've built up really good relationships with the local school nursery and the teacher there provides me with copies of her planning, which I can use as a reference when planning my own provision.

Sharon, owner/leader of a private nursery setting and currently on the long pathway to EYPS

I strive to ensure that the children have opportunity and access to a wide range of activities and resources that support each of the EYFS areas of learning. There is an abundance of natural materials and play resources that the children can access freely. We also plan for teacher-led activities and have a dedicated room for this, which makes it 'special' and focused for the different groups of children who use this with their Key Person. Our outdoor area is a reflection of the indoors with the widest possible provision. It is essentially an outdoor classroom. We have a sensory garden for growing, and watching small animals – this includes a wormery, hedgehog box and bird table. The outdoor role-play area includes a wooden 'house', which we adapt to the children's interests and needs. The barked area has a plastic canopy with tables and chairs that can be used for a whole range of table-top and small-group activities in all weather conditions. Our hard surface area has numbers, alphabetical letters and opportunities for physical development (wheeled equipment, bats and balls, etc). All our walls have visual display areas – including a 'feelings board', a clock, posters of mini-beasts, fruit and vegetables. We find that each child will make his or her own use of the resources that are available, and each member of the staff team is encouraged to create a balance of adult-led and child-led activities, monitoring their own effectiveness and practice in supporting their key children's learning.

Menna, EYP and manager of a pre-school offering sessional care

Having read of the work of Ferre Laevers, I am currently exploring how this impacts on my practice and setting. His ideas of children's deep engagement in learning, their well-being and adult involvement as indicators of quality provision certainly resonate with me. I also now work as an EYP tutor and so have opportunity to visit EYP candidates in their workplaces. I certainly then recognise the 'gut feeling' one has on entering a new setting, and am trying to quantify and define this for myself. I know that I expect to see children engaged in an activity to the extent that they are hardly aware of my presence as a 'stranger'. A recent visitor to my setting commented that she knew the children were engaged as they took barely any notice of her when she arrived or left. Effective learning is also, I believe, indicated by practitioners who are similarly involved in activity alongside children. Looking deeper, I believe all practitioners – led by an EYP – should be champions of their key children, and informed and eloquent about them, their abilities, needs or next steps.

Self-assessment task

We opened this chapter with reference to Standards 7 and 24 and you might like to reflect further here on how these EYPs are demonstrating *accountability for high quality provision and high expectations of each child* (CWDC, 2008, pp79–80). How might you strengthen your evidence for these Standards in your own practice?

C H A P T E R   S U M M A R Y

The focus in this chapter has been on the role of the EYP in children's learning, particularly the nature of their interactions with the children, and the central importance of the Key Person role has been identified. Seminal research and theory – such as that of Bruner on the scaffolding of learning by the adult (Bruner, 1978), that of Laevers' (1994) on children's engagement in learning, and the adult role in supporting this as developed in the EEL project (Pascal and Bertram, 2001), have all been outlined and highlighted. These are key to our understanding of those aspects of the EYP role as pedagogue, effectively supporting all children to learn and develop. The different types of interaction between practitioner and child have been discussed, especially in play situations, and an integrated pedagogical model (Wood, 2008) encouraged. You have had opportunity to reflect on a range of first-hand accounts from different EYPs and to think specifically about the EYPS Standards that relate to 'Effective Practice' (Standards 7–24). You should now feel empowered to think about the kind of evidence you might select to show how you meet these Standards.

Moving on

Our discussion of the EYP role in supporting learning and development has inevitably touched on Standard 16: *Engage in sustained shared thinking with children* (CWDC, 2008, p34) and in the next chapter there is opportunity to engage with this important aspect of effective Early Years pedagogy, to reflect on its theoretical and research base (Siraj-Blatchford *et al.*, 2002a) and to explore, through case study examples and practical tasks, why this is considered to be a defining aspect of the EYP's personal practice and one that they should effectively model to others.

FURTHER READING

Selleck, D (2006) Key persons in the Early Years Foundation Stage. *Early Education*, 50: 11–13.

Laevers, F (ed.) with Daems, M, De Bruyckere, G, Declerq, B, Moons, J, Silkens, K, Snoek, G and Van Kessel, M (2005) *Well-being and Adult Involvement in Care Settings. A Process-oriented Self-evaluation Instrument, A Manual*. Leuven, Belgium: Centre for Experiential Education, University of Leuven. Available online at: www.kindengezin.be/Images/ZikohandleidingENG_tcm149-50761.pdf.

Pascal, C and Bertram, A (2000) *The Effective Early Learning Project: Achievements and Reflections*. London: House of Commons, Available online at: www.publications.parliament.uk/pa/cm199900/cmselect/cmeduemp/386/0061406.htm (accessed 20 November 2009).

7 Sustained shared thinking

CHAPTER OBJECTIVES

The practitioner role in support of children's thinking skills is now clearly embedded both within the Early Years Professional Standards and within the Early Years Foundation Stage Framework. This chapter explores the concept of sustained shared thinking with children, and a range of strategies are suggested through which children's thinking and understanding can be developed and extended. This includes observing children's drawing and using the Mosaic Approach, which encourages a pedagogy of listening to children. It is argued that the capacity to engage in sustained shared thinking with children is core to effective Early Years pedagogy and is an aspect of the EYP role that should be both part of personal practice and modelled to colleagues. Examples of effective practice are shared to support reflective and practical tasks, which provide opportunity to gain a greater understanding of this aspect of the EYP role.

After reading this chapter you should be able to:
- critically appraise the concept of sustained shared thinking, and understand the theoretical and research context that underpins it;
- explore aspects of the EYP role that enable and facilitate sustained shared thinking with children;
- begin to apply an understanding of the above to your own role and practice.

The focus in this chapter is primarily on Standard 16, although there will be some relevance and application to a range of other Standards such as 7, 22, 24 and 25.

Introduction

Sustained shared thinking

The significance of adults and children engaging in 'sustained shared learning' was a key outcome arising out of the REPEY Report (Siraj-Blatchford *et al.*, 2002a) though, as noted, it is not actually a *new* concept as such, but – rather – a new name given to the value and potential of adult–child interactions. Standard 16 requires that the EYP *engages in sustained shared thinking with children*, with further guidance given that this involves *providing planned and seizing un-planned opportunities to improve children's thinking skills by engaging them in high quality verbal interactions* (CWDC, 2008, p34). Within the

EYFS Framework, there is specific guidance offered on this aspect of the practitioner role (DCSF, 2008d, 4.3). However, there is still widespread confusion about both the meaning of the term and how it is evidenced and, indeed, neither of these is without its challenge. When the authors surveyed a group of EYPs/those on training pathways about their understanding of sustained shared thinking (SST), the responses were varied:

> *It's when children invite practitioners to join their play, giving them the opportunity to ask open-ended questions which, in turn, gives children the opportunity to explain the thinking behind their play. The practitioners can then ask appropriate questions to encourage the children's thinking and move their understanding forward.*

> *At weekly circle time sessions, I ask the children to discuss what they have done/learned since last week.*

> *I like Marion Dowling's definition of sustained shared thinking as being like a good conversation with a friend. This involves sharing ideas and listening carefully to each other. This respectful style enables participants to learn from each other and to move forward with shared understanding.*

> *At my setting, we plan from our observations of children and always seek to listen and respond to the voice of the individual children.*

> *SST occurs quite naturally in our setting as children are encouraged to think and act independently. Practitioners ask for children's opinions and consult them. For instance, we recently consulted with them about changes to our life play area, which then became a cafe.*

> *I really try to encourage the children in my setting to ask questions and always do my best to answer the questions and look for ways to extend their learning by providing examples or activities to back up what we are talking about. For example, we might explore colour through colour mixing paint or adding food colouring to playdough and water. I find that if an activity is child led, the thinking can be extended for a long sustained period because the child is interested in it.*

REFLECTIVE TASK

- *Do any of the above definitions resonate with your own understanding of sustained shared thinking?*

- *Are there any with which you found yourself disagreeing? Why was this?*

The definitions offered above are typical of those within the Early Years workforce and do highlight the range of understandings and different emphases relating to Standard 16. For example, does the use of the word 'sustained' here mean that the learning takes place over time? Is the nature of 'shared' learning always and only about adult and child? Does it always include verbal interactions? It is from such questions that we turn to the REPEY Report (Siraj-Blatchford *et al.*, 2002a, p8), where, drawing on earlier work from Wells (1985), who referred to *collaborative meaning making*, sustained shared thinking was defined as *an episode in which two or more individuals 'work together' in an intellectual way to solve a problem, clarify a concept, evaluate activities, extend a narrative etc. Both parties must contribute to the thinking and it must develop and extend.* Other more succinct definitions include *situations where children's level of thinking is 'lifted' and becomes much deeper* (Chilvers, 2008, p19) – thus the 'sustained' element here is not simply about chronological time but allows for learning to penetrate and become accommodated within the child's memory. This can include child–child conversations. SST is, however, generally between a practitioner and child and, at the 2005 Training Advancement and Cooperation in Teaching Young Children (TACTYC, 2005, p1) Conference, is defined simply as 'engaging children in extra talk', beyond the routine and general level of conversations with them. One of the strongest definitions to date focuses on the cognitive process involved in SST and it is this that forms the focus of this chapter.

> *[In sustained shared thinking]* . . . *the cognitive construction [is]* . . . *mutual, where each party engages with the understanding of the other and learning is achieved through a process of reflexive co-construction.*
>
> (Siraj-Blatchford et al., 2002a, p10; Siraj-Blatchford and Sylva, 2004, p720)

Links with theory

You may like to look back at Chapter 2 at this point, as a number of theorists and thinkers have contributed to our developing understanding of SST within Early Years pedagogy. Vygotsky's (1978) work is seminal; his thinking on social interaction and the importance of a 'more knowledgeable other' in children's learning processes has been outlined and, while SST goes further than this in acknowledging the 'mutuality' of learning, nonetheless the interactional nature of effective learning is clearly rooted in this theory. Bruner's (1961) concept of 'scaffolding' – with the child as an active learner, actively supported by the adult – also underpins our understanding of SST, as does Rogoff's (2003) concept of guided participation. Lave and Wenger's (1991) understanding of 'situated learning' is particularly pertinent. They argue that the deepest learning is 'situated'; by this they mean that it is clearly embedded within a combination of activity, context and culture. Such learning is usually unintentional rather than deliberate, and positive social interaction and effective collaboration between 'learner' and 'teacher' (who may, in fact, be another child) are essential components of such situated learning. Vygotsky's influence is also seen in Schaffer's (1996) notion of 'joint involvement episodes' – though, for Schaffer, this was very much to do with the more knowledgeable adult passing this on to the receptive, interested, enquiring child. Contemporary understanding of SST focuses much more on mutual cognitive construction, or co-construction of meaning and learning.

More recently, there has been significant work on the connections between 'creativity' and thinking skills. Indeed, the EYFS (DCSF, 2008d, 4.3) emphasises such connections. Fisher (2002) believes that creative individuals are those who can generate ideas, strive for originality and are flexible in their thinking. Craft's significant work (2000) on 'Big C and little c' creativity defines the latter as the human capacity for resourcefulness, innovation and problem solving. Mayesky (1998) defined two kinds of thinking that produce solutions: *convergent* thinking, which results in a single answer to a question or problem; and *divergent* thinking, which opens issues up and results in a range of possible answers. Based on New Zealand's Early Childhood Curriculum, *Te Whāriki* (NZME, 1996), Carr (2001) suggests that the fundamental aim of Early Years pedagogy is to establish children's healthy dispositions for learning. She defines these dispositions (Carr, 2001, p23) as 'five domains':

1. taking an interest (in learning);

2. being involved (in learning);

3. persisting with difficulty and uncertainty;

4. communicating purposefully with others;

5. taking responsibility (for learning).

Opportunities for sustained shared learning include all these 'domains' and, for the EYP, offer much food for thought as we consider the importance of the adult role in communicating effectively and meaningfully with children, encouraging and stretching their thinking and understanding, and enhancing their problem-solving skills. Where children are motivated to learn, are deeply engaged in the learning process, and can persevere and express their needs through effective communication, there will usually be opportunities for sustained shared learning. Remember, such 'communication' need not be verbal and the following examples show three very young children engaged in activities that offer possibilities for sustained shared thinking.

CASE STUDY

Nia, aged 14 months, in a childminder's home setting

Unsupported, Nia – who has been walking for about a month – has lined up three soft toys against the wall and starts to feed them. In the playbox, she finds a soft brush, a plastic spoon and some ribbons. She appears to be trying to put the ribbon on one of the teddies, but is showing signs of frustration.

CASE STUDY

Krista, aged two years eight months, in a voluntary pre-school

Krista has been attending her local pre-school for two months and has settled fairly well but rarely volunteers any information or asks anything of her Key Person. What Krista likes doing at the moment is tying things up. She likes to wrap paper in elastic bands or sticky tape from the mark-making area, and uses the pipe cleaners to tie up clothes in the home corner. This morning, Krista finds a long piece of rope and is wrapping it round and round one of the posts in the outdoor area.

William, aged four years, in full day-care provision at a Children's Centre

William has been to visit Jodrell Bank telescope with his family at the weekend and comes into the Children's Centre on Monday morning, clutching a postcard and small model replica of the telescope in his hands. He is animated, and talks and talks to his Key Person about the trip, describing his 3-D trip with 'special glasses' to Mars, over Martian volcanoes and canyons.

REFLECTIVE TASK

- *What opportunities are presented in the above case studies for the practitioners working with Nia, Krista and William to engage in SST with them?*

- *What can EYPs do to remain more 'in tune' with opportunities for SST? How much more challenging is this when the children (as Nia and Krista) are not particularly seeking out their Key Person?*

Researching Effective Pedagogy in the Early Years (REPEY) (Siraj-Blatchford *et al.*, 2002a)

The REPEY study identified a clear correlation between opportunities for SST and the effectiveness and quality of children's learning, with the finding of the research team that *children who engage in sustained shared conversations are more likely to do well in school and life* (TACTYC, 2005, p1). As noted, the aim of the REPEY project was to identify the most effective pedagogical strategies used within the (then) Foundation Stage (QCA, 2000), with children from three to five years. From the intensive case studies conducted as part of the REPEY project, all settings and practitioners were found to give priority to children's social development, but the project's evidence found that *those settings which see cognitive and social development as complementary achieve the best profile in terms of child outcomes* (Siraj-Blatchford *et al.*, 2002a, p10).

The research team investigated specific aspects of practice in order to identify factors that enabled children to make greater developmental progress. One of these aspects of practice was adult–child verbal interactions. We established earlier that children's motivation and positive dispositions to learning are critical to its effectiveness, and the REPEY team found this to be conversely true of the effective educator – where *learning is achieved through reflexive 'co-construction' . . . Both parties are* involved *and, for the resultant learning to be worthwhile, the content should be in some way* instructive (Siraj-Blatchford *et al.*, 2002a, p10). In their analysis of the adult's pedagogical interactions, the REPEY research team divided the 'cognitive codes' into three separate types, one of which is defined as *sustained shared thinking interactions* (Siraj-Blatchford *et al.*, 2002a, p144).

These include concepts we have already discussed in Chapter 6: scaffolding, extending, discussing, modelling and playing. As an EYP engaging children in SST, it is important that you remain motivated and involved in the learning that is taking place, committed to using diverse strategies to support effective learning in your setting.

Self-assessment task

The following questions posed within the EYFS (DCSF, 2008d, 4.3) thoughtfully support effective practice and you are encouraged to use these here to help you identify opportunities for SST with the children in your setting. Note your ideas in the table below.

Ask yourself:	Think: How might I put this into practice in my setting?
How do I get involved in the thinking process with children?	
How do I develop and maintain my awareness of the children's interests and understandings, and work together with the children to develop an idea or skill?	
How do I show genuine interest to children, offer them encouragement, clarify what they are thinking and ask open questions?	
How do I show genuine interest to children, offer them encouragement, clarify what they are thinking and ask open questions?	

The reflective practitioner

Shortly, we will look in more detail at some specific ways these interactions can be used by the EYP to develop children's thinking but, before we do, it is important not only to focus on pragmatic strategies but to consider again the important principle of reflection that underpins effective Early Years pedagogy. Clarke (2007) defines reflective practice as the fundamental building block of sustained shared learning, with other blocks including staff knowledge and training, the establishment of effective trusting relationships, and practitioners who show genuine enthusiasm and enjoyment in children's achievement. In giving her book the title *Sustaining Shared Thinking*, Clarke (2007) is emphasising the importance of a reflective stance in seeking to embed this crucial aspect of pedagogy into continuous EYFS practice.

The work of Schön (1983) on reflective practice is well documented, and the distinction he makes between reflection *in* and reflection *on* practice is highly relevant for the EYP role, and links directly to Standards 38 and 39. Schön is credited with bringing reflection *into the centre of what professionals do*, empowering practitioners with a tool that enables them to be both *connoisseurs and critics* (Smith, 2009, p3). Schön's notion of *reflection-in-action* is sometimes described as 'thinking on our feet' and involves allowing ourselves to go with a particular experience, connecting with our feelings and seeking – almost unconsciously – to apply existing knowledge (both experiential and theoretical) to the experience. We do not do this, however, with closed minds about 'textbook' theory but rather, drawing on what's gone before and marrying this to the current situation, we are part of an ongoing *grounding of professional knowledge* (Usher *et al.*, 1997).

This process of thinking on our feet then becomes linked to Schön's 'reflection-on-action', which is done after the event or experience, and allows time to explore why we did what we did and what factors were at play. The two processes are connected and enable us, as practitioners, to develop a set of questions and ideas about our role and practice. Thus, this 'repertoire of reflection' (Smith, 2009, p4) enables us to engage positively and constructively with a situation or experience – even one that is, to all appearances, challenging and difficult. It allows us to build up a collection of images, ideas, examples and actions that can be drawn upon in the future. Arguably, reflective practice is about our engagement with a process of sustained thinking – whether or not it is shared with others. Menna's experience in the following case study illustrates this very effectively.

CASE STUDY

Menna, EYP and manager of a pre-school offering sessional care

As an EYP I am committed to being a reflective practitioner and evaluating what happened and what I did about it. Recently, I overheard the following conversation as I was observing a group of three and four year olds with a worm they had dug up. As I listened, I heard one of our more able, and influential, four year olds state dogmatically, 'Worms turn into butterflies you know.' I was surprised at this comment, especially the confidence with which it was delivered. Why has she got it wrong? (I mean to say we have posters with the life cycle of a butterfly; we have read The Very Hungry Caterpillar, played the game and done the jigsaw.) What should I do? I can't have all these children thinking worms turn into butterflies! Should I tell them she is wrong and I am right? What would that do to her self-esteem? Would it encourage the others in the group to volunteer answers in the future? In a split second these thoughts race through my mind. Through all these questions, I sensed myself 'reflecting in practice'.

'Are you all sure about that?' I asked, 'What else do you know about butterflies?' As the conversation progressed, and others contributed, it became clear that the children knew that caterpillars turn into butterflies, what they were not sure about was what worms turned into. The original speaker was convinced that they too turn into butterflies. It is definitely easier to show what does happen with the use of 'information' books than it is to show what does not happen. No one has produced a book or online source that says worms do not turn into butterflies!

As the interest of the children turned to how the worm moved and whether they could find any more, the moment had passed. At circle time we read The Very Hungry

Caterpillar (Eric Carle), we looked at a poster showing the life cycle of a butterfly and I introduced the word 'metamorphosis' – the children love long words! In my reflection on action later I talked with other staff and friends about the incident. I believe that children learn best by experience, which I could not immediately directly offer, so one option was to set up a wormery.

This experience enabled me to consider my understanding of young children's learning, which had prevented me from telling them the 'answer' (that I was right and they were wrong) – this was the focus for my reflection on practice. I had used the children's knowledge to inform our discussion, and to construct together a theory about the world of worms, caterpillars and butterflies. We had considered possibilities together and while the question of what worms turn into was still unresolved for some of them, I had been able to offer my understanding that worms just go on getting bigger; maybe the wormery will help the learning be embedded?

REFLECTIVE TASK

Here, in writing about her experience, Menna is reflecting on action although she is also able to identify how she also reflected in action.

- *Pick out here all the reflective questions that Menna asked herself in action. What was the consequence of these on her actions?*

- *How did Menna engage in a process of reflection on action, and how did this enable her to develop her own thinking about her role and practice?*

- *What do you think might have happened in this scenario if Menna had not taken a reflective approach?*

- *Can you think of any comparable examples from your own practice of reflection in and/or on practice?*

Listening to children

SST starts with effective listening to children (Standard 27). Such listening involves far more than the physical process of hearing. Egan (2009) suggests it is crucial that Early Years practitioners develop a *listening pedagogy* and become skilled in *learning conversations*. As an EYP, at the 'cutting edge' of leading effective practice, role modelling such skills is an important aspect of your work. Starting with babies, this *listening pedagogy* includes *mutually rewarding emotional engagement* with the responsible adult *tuned into children's movements, rhythms and vocalisations* (Parker-Rees, 2007, p5). Such engagement enables the baby to engage in play, relate to peers, and develop independence and a strong sense of self. If early learning is to do with the development of children's learning capacity, then the practitioner should enable even the youngest children to communicate their own ideas (Palmer and Doyle, 2004, cited in Clarke, 2007).

The Mosaic Approach to listening to young children was developed in the early 2000s by Clark and Moss (2005). Drawing on fieldwork data from Sweden, and inspired by the Reggio Emilia notion that the child has *100 languages* (Malaguzzi, cited in Fillipini and Vecchi, 1997, p3) through which they can communicate, the Mosaic Approach acknowledges the child as *co-constructor of meaning*, and seeks to integrate verbal with visual, tuning in to the voice of the child in order to *gain deeper understanding of children's lives* (Clark and Moss, 2005, p8). Rinaldi (2001, p4) describes a *pedagogy of listening*, which she defines as the *basis for any learning relationship*.

Influenced by the concept of 'participatory appraisal' (empowerment of the weakest in any society) (Pottier, 1997), Clark and Moss (2005, p10) wanted to explore how adults and children can *make meaning together*. The Mosaic Approach seeks to allow expression to Article 12 of the 1989 United Nations (UN) Convention on the Rights of the Child – the right of the child to form views and express these freely in all matters affecting them (UN, 1989). Encouraging a reflective and reflexive stance to practice, the focus is on the child's actual *lived* experience and their own perspective on those experiences. This multi-method approach uses discussion with children, photographs they have freely taken, child-led tours of the setting, and children's maps, drawings and other representational work to supplement practitioner-led observations and parent interviews, and thus create a *co-constructed* picture of the child's world. Tanagh, an experienced EYP and room leader with three to four year olds in a private nursery is mentor to Dan, from another private setting nearby, who is currently preparing for EYPS. Dan asks Tanagh about her experience of using the Mosaic Approach within her setting:

> Dan: *My tutor talked about this approach at my last training session and we have a reading extract about it. But how does it work in practice? I mean I know it's important to listen to children's views but are we also supposed to act on these every time?*

> Tanagh: *It's a common misconception that using the Mosaic Approach is like 'child power', children taking over all the decision making. It's not like that at all. The original idea is that it's about getting the child's views and understanding what his opinions and feelings are. What is really important is to take time analysing the information that you get from children – from their photographs, drawings, discussion with them, and work out how you can best use that information.*

> Dan: *How have you been able to do that?*

> Tanagh: *Well, recently, staff had been feeling that the layout of the indoor learning base was wrong somehow. The book corner and mark-making area were hardly being accessed and the mark-making resources were hardly visible to the children in any case; they were kind of hidden behind the life play area. I thought it was important to get the children's perspectives here so before we as staff made any tangible plans, we discussed this with the children in circle time and encouraged those who wanted to draw pictures of what they'd like in the room to do those for us. I then invited Millie and Joe, two of our three year olds who tend not to take*

part much even in small-group discussion, to walk round our room with me, telling me: what they really like in our resources, what activities they like best, what they hardly ever use, etc. It really was amazing what we learned from the children. Millie particularly said more on that walk than we've ever known her say before. We learned of her favourite jigsaw, a book that she also has at home that's also in our book corner and that she has a cat who's been poorly so went to the vet. We are wondering if our life play area should be changed into a vet's practice and ask Millie to help us design the layout of this based on her recent visit.

Dan: *So – it really is a 'partnership' thing, with the adults interpreting the children's ideas, perspectives, preferences and insights in order to develop and improve practice?*

Tanagh: *You've got it!*

REFLECTIVE TASK

Think how the children and Tanagh here are co-constructing the changes. While this is not in itself sustained shared thinking, important relationships are forged here that are fundamental to SST.

How would you explain and exemplify the 'pedagogy of listening' that is the Mosaic Approach to a colleague?

Children's mark making

Drawing is one of Reggio Emilia's *many languages* (Malaguzzi, cited in Fillipini and Vecchi, 1997, p3), used by children to talk about their worlds, both to themselves and to others. Part fine motor skill development – with hand–eye co-ordination a key component – and part play, Alley (2007) sees drawing as a reflection of young children's inner schematic representations (as outlined in Chapter 2). Matthews (1999, p4) concurs that, for younger children, mark making provides opportunity to explore the lines and curves of trajectory and enclosure schemas, for instance. However, for older children between the ages of three and four, he views drawing as *located within a family of expressing and symbolic actions [which they] use fluently*. He goes on to describe the *interpersonal arena between caregiver and infant* that is core to young children's drawings. Early Years practitioners, thus, should take children's mark making seriously and look for opportunities to interact with children about their drawings. However, caution is urged in over-analysing children's drawings without any reference to the child's own narrative, and Ring's research (2001) shows how, all too frequently, the role of drawing in children's learning is misunderstood. Emphasising the interrelational aspect of drawing, Ring (2001, p14) urges practitioners to explore *the relationship between drawing as communication and drawing as art*.

It is this emphasis on drawing as *communication* that is pertinent here in our discussion on sustained shared thinking as it is one possible meaningful way of engaging children's thinking. Mark-making opportunities, then, are seen to be an important aspect of provision for young children from the time they are able to hold a 'mark maker' of some kind, as these allow for expression of a young child's developing thinking. *Children draw pictures and tell a story at the same time; they act a role and create lines as they go along . . . in a dynamic meeting between the child's inner life of emotions and thoughts and [her] external world* (Lindqvist, 2001, p8). As an EYP, you are encouraged to 'tune in' to children's drawings and what children tell you – visually and/or orally – about their lives through the drawings. Think how you can use these to encourage children's thinking through the shared creation of meaning.

CASE STUDY

Jillian, preparing for EYP assessment, works in the pre-school of an independent school

Jillian is key worker to Olly, aged four. Look at Olly's drawing here.

Jillian is at hand to listen to Olly talking about his drawing.

> They are clouds at the top and the rain is coming out. It's falling out and down and connecting and going into the drain. Look that's a water pistol!

As Jillian listens to Olly's narrative, she recognises that he is making sense of his world and has a current fascination for water. She recalls other observations she has carried out on Olly, and recognises his keen interest in lines. He loves to draw lines; when he writes his name with 2 'l's in it, he makes these very long, often down to the bottom of the page. In the outdoor area, he assembles the boxes in a long line to make a train and also creates a long 'rolling chute' – though he does include a wonderful 45-degree angle in this. Jillian recognises this as a trajectory schema and applies herself to thinking how she can provide further opportunities for Olly to build on his current interests.

REFLECTIVE TASK

- *Who else might Jillian consult about Olly's current interests and how these can be developed?*

- *What further opportunities might she offer to Olly to extend his current level of thinking?*

- *In particular, is there anything else in this drawing that you would want to follow up?*

Leading practice in sustained shared thinking

Because there is strong reference to the concept of SST within the EYFS guidance documentation (DCSF, 2008d, 2008e), you may well be able to access appropriate and helpful training on this aspect of practice which, in turn, you can cascade to colleagues. As we have seen, it was Siraj-Blatchford and her team whose work was the catalyst for this (the RFPEY Report, 2002a) and she continues to make a significant contribution to both our understanding and application of the pedagogical base for SST. In 2005, in her keynote address to TACTYC's Annual Conference, Siraj-Blatchford identified a range of strategies that will enable lead practitioners to engage children in SST. These include what she describes as positive questioning, and include both questions and 'open statements', which, while not technically questions, leave an appropriate 'space' for the child to respond, without feeling obliged to do so. Children need opportunities to ask and answer different types of question. The more open ended the better for encouraging their thinking. Such positive questions include:

- I'm not sure, what do you think?

- That's a really interesting idea . . .

- I like what you have done there, could you . . .

- Have you seen what child x has done?

- I wondered why you had . . .

- I've never thought about that before . . .

- You've really made me think . . .

- What would happen if we did . . .

Such questioning needs to be done skilfully, appropriately and in the right context. Look how Danni and Andrew are co-constructing meaning in this scenario.

CASE STUDY

Danni, preparing for EYPS assessment and assistant leader of a sessional pre-school

Part of the Key Person role in my setting includes responsibility for regular observations of our key children. Andrew is three years old and is one of my key children; he started at our pre-school about four months ago. From the outset, I established Andrew's interests and learning preference: he likes cars, trains, puzzles, role play and one-to-one games with adults. He did not settle well at first and often went to the telephone in the corner to 'phone Mummy to pick me up'. I believe the essence of effective Key Person work is good communication with the child and feel I first connected with Andrew when, about a month after he started at the group, we were chatting and he volunteered that 'I need cars, running cars and faster cars. Lightening McQueen cars. I need Thomas and I need Roary . . . I need all the other ones, too. Lightening McQueen cars are at Tesco's, Daddy's new car, Daddy's got a new car.' Here I noted that Andrew was using 'the vocabulary focused upon objects and people that are of particular interest' to him from the CLL programme in the EYFS.

The next time Andrew attended the group, I provided a box of 'vehicles' and a large sheet of paper on which I'd drawn the first part of lines – possibly representing a route. Andrew was very excited about these: 'You've got Thomas things!' He did show significant interest in lining up the cars and letting them follow the line on the paper so I decided to follow his trajectory schema by modelling to him how vehicles can make tracks in wet sand. Soon after this, Mum sent in some of his favourite cars from home and this led to a fascinating development in his play, which I was able to observe and contribute to with open questions and encouragers. Andrew took some cars outside and hid them in the snow. 'They need snow on them, sand on them makes them smaller! Look this one has got pipes . . . That's right, pipes in the back. They have water in them. It's the boost! Come out of the little back, the – er – metal. It comes from the boost of the pipes – er – water in it.'

Through sustained involvement in Andrew's play I believe I played a key role not only in his settling in and developing his self-confidence but also in his cognitive development. I also learned so much from this play. I believe I empowered him in many ways – but he also helped me to see how I am both teacher and learner. I was able to document this as part of Andrew's Learning Journey and share it in a staff training session.

- *How is Danni demonstrating her capacity for SST with Andrew?*

- *What kind of questions do you think Danni would have asked Andrew about his interests?*

- *How are Danni and Andrew co-constructing learning here?*

- *How is Danni demonstrating leadership of practice here?*

Siraj-Blatchford (2005) identified a range of skills and qualities that lead practitioners can develop to support SST with children. These are shown in column 1 of the table below, with a brief explanation where required. In column 2 you are encouraged to think of an example of when you might demonstrate this in your role and practice. Each of these will relate to Standard 16, but you are also encouraged to link your response to other Standards in column 3.

Strategy (linked to Standard 16)	How might you demonstrate this?	Links to other EYP Standards
Tuning in – listening carefully to what is being said, observing the children's non-verbal indicators and actions		
Genuineness – showing through eye contact, nodding, smiling and your undivided attention that you are truly interested in the child		
Respecting the child's own decisions and choices, and inviting them to tell you more about these		
Suggesting – respectfully offering alternative ways of doing things		
Reminding – of something the child said earlier		
Encouragement to further thinking – for instance, *You have really thought hard about putting a roof cover on your den but where are you going to put the door?*		
Offering an alternative viewpoint – for instance, about a character in a well-loved story: *Maybe the . . .*		

Strategy (linked to Standard 16)	How might you demonstrate this?	Links to other EYP Standards
Speculating (an extension of the above) – offer a specific example of what might happen		
Reciprocating – *What a good thing you built that den. Now it's starting to rain we can all go inside and stay dry.*		
Modelling thinking (perhaps over snack or in circle time) – *I need to think very hard. When I go home from nursery, I must remember to call at the Post Office to buy some stamps and then at the supermarket because I need something for my tea. I left some washing on the line – what am I going to do if it rains this afternoon?*		
Recapping – summarising what the child has said but in your own words: *So you have decided to . . . and you think that . . .*		
Self-disclosure/offering your own experience – *I like to grow tomatoes at home and when the baby tomatoes appear I touch them gently every day while I water them. I think that helps them to grow.*		
Clarifying ideas – *Right, Anna, you think this stone will sink if we put it in the water. Why do you think that?*		

C H A P T E R   S U M M A R Y

We have explored the meaning of 'sustained shared thinking' and established that it starts with effective listening to children, from babyhood onwards. We have seen that, following the outcomes of the REPEY Report (Siraj-Blatchford *et al.*, 2002a), this has come to be seen as one of the indicators of quality practice and has clear links to effective practice. Some of the challenges in definition have been identified and we have considered a range of strategies, such as children's drawings and the Mosaic Approach, that can be used successfully to support SST. The importance of its being rooted in reflective practice cannot be over-stated. Case study examples enabled you to apply some of the theoretical elements to practice, and the chapter concluded with a practical task based on some of Siraj-Blatchford's (2005) suggestions of skills and attributes to support SST with children.

Moving on

We have seen that SST with children is a key quality indicator of effective practice (REPEY, Siraj-Blatchford *et al.*, 2002). The notion of 'quality indicators' is developed in the next chapter, and you will have opportunity to reflect on a range of aspects of practice that signpost effective settings. These are considered in relation to a range of EYP Standards.

FURTHER READING

Clarke, J (2008) Fostering young children's thinking skills. *Teaching Expertise.* Available online at: www.teachingexpertise.com/articles/fostering-young-childrens-thinking-skills-3193.

Jolley, RP (2010) *Children and Pictures: Drawing and Understanding.* Chichester: Blackwell (Chapter 5: Children's understanding of the dual nature of pictures).

8 Evaluating effective practice

CHAPTER OBJECTIVES

This chapter considers how EYPs are concerned with effecting change and raising the quality of Early Years provision, and reflects on the underlying rationale for this role. The concept of 'quality provision' is seen to be subject to differing interpretations within the field of Early Years practice, and various quality indicators may be used to contribute to judgements about the effectiveness of practice. However, EYPs may have various perceptions about the quality of provision in their settings and consider diverse views on priorities for developing practice; these may well be highly contextualised. EYPs affirm their own perspectives and concerns about effectiveness, which are derived from a sound understanding of the outcomes of *Every Child Matters* (ECM) (DfES, 2004) and the four EYFS Principles (DCSF, 2008a), and which are framed by the EYP Standards (CWDC, 2008). The case studies in this chapter illustrate how EYPs have developed practice in their settings. While EYPs may face challenges when seeking to raise the quality of provision, it is important to tackle these with sensitivity, courage and determination in order to promote children's longer-term outcomes.

After reading this chapter you should be able to:
- deepen your understanding of how effective provision in the Early Years can reduce inequalities that currently exist between different groups of children;
- critically analyse the concept of 'quality provision' and explore some of the indicators that might inform judgements about the effectiveness of practice;
- examine how EYPs can act as advocates for children's rights to access to high-quality provision.

Standards 24, 31, 33 and 38 are most relevant in this chapter, although others are also referred to and signposted.

Introduction

In Chapter 1, we considered how the key elements of the four overarching EYFS Principles can support practitioners to reflect, evaluate and develop their practice (DCSF, 2008a). These elements are of particular significance for EYPs, who are expected to promote the Principles, and lead and support others to implement them in their everyday provision (S1) (CWDC, 2008). Case studies in previous chapters have demonstrated ways in which EYPs have embedded the EYFS Principles into the fabric of their setting's provision, both within the context of their own practice and that of others whom they lead and support. These serve to illustrate how EYPs are *catalysts for change and innovation . . . raising the quality of early years provision* (CWDC, 2008, p5). S24, which expects EYPs to *be accountable for the delivery of high quality provision* (CWDC, 2008, p43), is directly concerned with EYPs' remit to improve the quality of provision. In this chapter, we explore how EYPs can take steps to develop and maintain high-quality provision.

At the outset, it is important to stress that the term 'quality' is in fact quite a slippery concept within the context of Early Years provision and practice. As we noted in Chapter 1, the widespread application of the term 'quality provision' within Early Years practice assumes that everyone concerned with the subject readily shares the same understanding of its determining factors; however, Elfer *et al.* (2003) suggest that its meaning is dependent on different priorities and concerns, and we offer here an exploration of some different interpretations and applications of this term.

Fundamentally, in seeking to develop the quality of provision, the EYP needs to ensure that the aims of such development are recognised and endorsed by those who will be affected by their implementation. Equally, it is important to understand that the process of development is shaped by the perceptions of others who are concerned with the setting's provision (Siraj-Blatchford and Manni, 2007). Therefore, effective communication and collaborative review of policy and practice facilitate the process of raising the quality of provision, and support EYPs in managing and adapting that process where necessary (S38) (CWDC, 2008). We start, though, by reviewing the underlying need for raising the quality of provision, which is embedded in current Early Years national policy.

The importance of effective Early Years provision

It is now widely recognised that high-quality Early Years provision can have a profound impact on children's future outcomes and help to overcome disadvantage in the early stages of their lives (Siraj-Blatchford *et al.*, 2002a; Melhuish, 2004; DCSF, 2009d). Consequently, since 1997, the government has sought to improve the provision experienced by young children in their Early Years, as this period in their lives offers unique opportunities for their learning and development. Significant gaps in the development of young children from different backgrounds within society have already emerged by the time children are five years old and can become embedded within intergenerational patterns of inequality (Feinstein, 2003). By this young age, children residing in the most disadvantaged local authorities are far less likely to be developing well than their counterparts from other areas, and these children can subsequently find it difficult to 'catch up' with their peers (Cabinet Office, 2009; DCSF, 2009e).

There have been a number of references already (particularly in Chapter 4) to the key role played by parents in supporting their children's early development. However, this role is so fundamental to children's future outcomes that it cannot be over-emphasised and is particularly relevant to any discussion about quality provision. Of particular importance here is the supporting role of EYPs in working constructively with those parents who hold negative perceptions of education. These are likely to be derived from their own poor experiences of educational provision, and it is vital that these views are not successively transmitted to their own child. Through building strong and respectful relationships, EYPs can work with parents to counteract those factors that can lead to early gaps emerging in children's development, thus preventing greater inequalities emerging between some children and their more advantaged peers in later life (DCSF, 2009f). EYPs *think child* (Feinstein *et al.*, 2007) – that is, they acknowledge parents' own perspectives about their children and, by building strong and respectful relationships, encourage parents to become more involved in their child's learning and development. S31 (CWDC, 2008) describes how EYPs understand the significance of reaching out to parents and how they appreciate when parents may be in need of appropriate levels of nurturing. Through deep engagement and respectful dialogue with parents, EYPs can start to turn around the cycle of disadvantage and observe the transformation of parents' and children's experiences at a key period in their lives.

PRACTICAL TASK

This task builds on the reflective and practical tasks concerning parents that you undertook in Chapter 4 (see pages 60, 61, 63 and 64). You should refer to your responses to those tasks before proceeding. If you have not already completed them, it is advisable you do so first before proceeding with this task.

This task is concerned with quality improvement in the setting's work with parents. You are encouraged to reflect on aspects of practice in your setting and then consider your response, noting your ideas in the following table.

Setting's actions that are concerned with parents	We do this already	This is developing	We need to do more	How do I know/ demonstrate this? (Consider any supporting evidence for your written tasks)
Our physical space is designed to encourage parents to spend time at the setting				
A member of staff leads on parental involvement in learning and actively works to promote it				
All parents regularly share their own observations of what children say and do at home				
Parents' observations are used to plan future learning in the setting and at home				

Setting's actions that are concerned with parents	We do this already	This is developing	We need to do more	How do I know/ demonstrate this? (Consider any supporting evidence for your written tasks)
Parents are given regular support for learning at home (e.g. activities/ equipment regularly shared between home and the setting)				
We have strategies in place to try to reach parents who are not taking part in what is offered				
We have good knowledge of where to find support for our parents locally (e.g. housing advice)				
Parents are involved in offering training and information to other parents about children's learning				
We have a clear 'transition' strategy – to support children and parents moving on to Reception				
Your own idea				

Source: adapted from Wheeler and Connor (2009, p110)

When you have completed this task, you may find it helpful to share your response with a colleague or your mentor. By explaining and sharing your ideas in this way, you can develop your thinking about the subject. This task might also be used as a basis for developing a presentation to parents, colleagues or for a Local Authority event. It is recommended that you date the entries you make in the table and then return to it at another time. By dating the actions you are taking, you can build a realistic picture of how much time you might spend on developing an aspect of practice.

In the policy document *Next Steps for Early Learning and Childcare: Building on the 10-year Strategy* (DCSF, 2009e, p10), the government reports that the results of the 2008 Foundation Stage Profile (FSP) reveal an improvement, for the first time, in bridging the gap between children living in the most disadvantaged areas and those in other areas. The number of children overall achieving a *good level of development* had risen by 4 per cent compared with the previous year. The greatest gap in children's achievement in these FSP results was seen in the communication, language and literacy scales. The strategic implementation of the programme *Every Child a Talker* (DCSF, 2008l) was highlighted in this report as key to reducing the gap in children's language scores by developing their communication skills. This programme, which is matched to the EYFS (DCSF, 2008a) and intended for use in Early Years settings, therefore represents another measure of effectiveness, or quality improvement.

REFLECTIVE TASK

- *Are you familiar with government or local authority materials that are currently available?*

- *Do you know how to locate and access the materials, if needed?*

- *Are practitioners in your setting familiar with and confident about the latest materials available?*

- *Do parents understand the programmes or strategies in use in your setting and know how they could be involved with these?*

- *Are children involved in decisions to adopt programmes or strategies that seek to promote their learning and development?*

- *Which EYP Standards are relevant to this task?*

The Early Years Foundation Stage Profile (EYFS Profile)

Outcomes based on the above data from the FSP, which is now known as the Early Years Foundation Stage Profile (EYFS Profile) (QCA/DCSF, 2008), are derived from a summative assessment that is a statutory requirement (DCSF, 2008a). The EYFS Profile draws principally on practitioners' observations and assessments of each child's achievements in all six areas of learning and development against 13 assessment scales. These judgements about a child should also incorporate information gained from discussions with their parents and others who have been involved with the child in the previous year. Parents are entitled to receive a copy of the profile. Local authorities (LAs) are charged with monitoring and moderating the EYFS Profile judgements to ensure consistency of assessment practice (DCSF, 2008a). Profile data is collected by LAs, who in turn submit it to the DCSF. As well as an information source for children's Year 1 teacher, therefore, the profile becomes the first statutory assessment of children's achievement. This is significant for Early Years Practitioners, as, even though they may not be involved in its formal completion, its outcomes provide a measure that informs future Early Years policy and practice.

However, while this formal assessment may be welcomed by LAs and government as a valuable source of data that serves to 'benchmark' children's achievement in their final year of the EYFS, the Profile has not been universally welcomed. For example, Moyles (2010, p28) argues that it reinforces a construct of *child development as the basis for early year's pedagogy*. Moyles points out that adopting a standard set of scale points to determine where a child may fit works against the concept of the EYFS theme 'the Unique Child', (DCSF, 2008a). This guiding theme requires practitioners to view children individually, rather than through a predetermined set of scale points, which are not suited to all children. Moreover, if we accept that all six areas of Learning and Development *must be delivered through planned, purposeful play* (DCSF, 2008a, p11), then we should also consider Moyles' (2010, p28) view that *play is the curriculum and not an occasional adjunct*. In other words, if we accept that play is the main form of children's activity, as previously explored in Chapters 2, 3 and 5, then we should consider the process of learning that takes place within this form, perhaps over some period of time.

REFLECTIVE TASK

Moyles (2010) calls for the development of shared understandings about play and the use of a common language to encapsulate children's learning that takes place within play, so that it can be communicated to others in a meaningful and useful way.

- *Reflect on how you communicate with children, parents and colleagues about children's learning within play.*

- *How do you ensure the provision of high-quality play environments in your setting?*

- *How do you encourage other practitioners to develop and maintain high-quality play environments?*

- *Are outdoor as well as indoor play environments subject to consistent monitoring and evaluation?*

A further concern about the Profile is that it is structured in a way that expects practitioners to record achievements within discrete areas of leaning and development; yet none of these areas is expected to be delivered in isolation from the others (DCSF, 2008a). Smidt (2009, p113) notes that practitioners who are using the Profile may plan activities with a predetermined learning outcome in mind in order to make judgements about that outcome so they can 'tick a box'. Smidt warns that this may not match the child's intended learning outcome and could work against the EYFS Learning and Development requirements, which state that practitioners should consider children's needs, interests and stages of development when planning a challenging and enjoyable experience across all six areas of Learning and Development (DCSF, 2008a).

At present, the completion of the Profile is a requirement – and viewed as an indicator of quality – so there is little choice over its use. However, the points expressed above illustrate some of the concerns that can surround the imposition of formal systems that are incorporated without due regard for the normal ethos of established practice. If practitioners see little value in the outcomes of a quality improvement measure, or have no confidence in the way it is conducted, then any perceived benefits could be out-weighed by the negative impact of the overall process. It is important that EYPs consider carefully the views of all those in the setting, so that everyone feels involved in the process and their concerns are heard. However, this does not mean that quality indicators have no place in practice. If they are applied in a manageable way that complements everyday practice, they can enrich understanding about children's learning and development, and contribute to the effectiveness of provision. The following case studies illustrate how different EYPs are using quality indicators that are responsive to children's learning. Consider the views expressed by the EYPs in the examples below and then record what you think are important quality indicators or measures of effectiveness in the following practical task.

CASE STUDY

Fiona, an EYP and Children's Centre manager

We base a large element of quality on observing the children's play and listening to the children's voices. I believe best Early Years practice should always be evolving, and everyone should be involved in new ideas and initiatives to excite the children. The best ideas often stem from observing a child in play and running with their concept; developing their play by providing resources and time for them.

I have also found a good gauge of quality to work alongside the EYFS and ECM outcomes as they both set clear objectives and statements that need to be achieved. They create a clear foundation for quality that you can build upon with innovative practice, for without clear foundations innovative practice will fail.

CASE STUDY

Pam, EYP and a childminder

I believe a key 'quality indicator' within Early Years practice is knowledgeable practitioners who know why they are doing things. For example, a setting may have a good settling-in procedure for new children but if practitioners do not understand the reasons behind this then they may not use it effectively and the new child may have greater difficulty settling in easily.

CASE STUDY

Judith, manager of a pre-school playgroup and currently on the long pathway to EYPS

I believe that the most important quality indicator is happy and confident children who make good developmental progress.

CASE STUDY *continued*

I also believe that the qualifications of the staff have a significant impact on the provision provided in a setting. Staff who recognise the importance of constantly reflecting and evaluating provision and participate in continuous personal professional development have a positive impact on children's learning and development. Continuous evaluation of provision is vital to improve outcomes for the children who attend.

Studying has ensured I have constantly reflected on my practice to ensure it is 'quality'. I have questioned my personal attitudes and beliefs, and assessed my current knowledge and skills, identifying areas for development. I have also considered how my practice impacts on children's learning and development. Having a better understanding of how children learn and valuing them as unique individuals has ensured I provide appropriate, 'quality', learning experiences, and this has resulted in the children learning through play, which interests them and which they enjoy.

CASE STUDY

Becky, at the point of EYPS validation and assistant manager at a Children's Centre

I believe quality is shaped by several factors starting with government, then managers, practitioners, parents and carers, but mainly by the children. If children do not respond to areas of provision, then it is not offering quality opportunities; children's play is the main indicator of quality provision.

CASE STUDY

Dawn, an EYP in a community pre-school playgroup

'Quality' is a safe, stimulating and inviting setting where children and adults can enjoy spending time. Indicators include warm and caring staff – although there is now an expectation that staff are highly qualified, this does not always mean that they are warm and caring. The ethos of the setting is hard to define. It is probably friendly staff, busy and engaged children. Evidence that the children are valued, pictures displayed on the walls, evidence that staff are listening to children and engaging in stimulating conversations (sustained shared thinking). Child-led activities – but with supportive adults and strong links between the setting and home. Local authority guidelines, consultants, own reading, degree course, and experiences of seeing other settings in practice.

Allana, an EYP and manager of a private nursery

Quality is shown in reflective settings that encourage children to develop strong and healthy relationships that allow them freedom to explore from the safety of the 'secure base', gradually developing independence and autonomy in their learning.

When you have considered the above case studies, which describe EYPs' different use of quality indicators, you are encouraged to reflect on the practice in your setting. Then record in the table below what you think are the key quality indicators within Early Years practice. Add any EYP Standards that you think are relevant.

Quality indicators of Early Years practice	Relevant EYP Standards

Ofsted

Early Years settings are subject to external assessment of their quality by the Office for Standards in Education, Children's Services and Skills (Ofsted), an independent government department that has responsibility for the inspection and regulation of registered Early Years settings and childcare provision. It reviews the setting's own self-evaluation form and, following the visit to a setting, provides reports about its provision. The reports are structured according to a set criteria for determining and regulating the quality of provision. These criteria are principally underpinned by the EYFS Framework (DCSF, 2008a) and the five outcomes of *Every Child Matters* (DfES, 2004). Ofsted's reports, which are placed in the public domain and accessible on its website, contain its graded judgements about the quality of a setting's provision (Ofsted, 2010). Its conclusions can be highly influential – for example, affecting parents' decisions about the choice of Early Years provision for their children. Details of Ofsted's website are included at the end of this chapter. You may find it helpful to look through some examples of Ofsted reports on Early Years settings that are available on its website, including the one for your setting.

The Early Childhood Environmental Rating Scale Extension (ECERS-E)

While Ofsted's role fulfils the purpose of monitoring provision at a broad level, its reports are not generally in sufficient detail to *act as an audit tool for local authorities to rigorously assess quality standards . . . or to offer centres . . . specific guidance on how to improve* (Mathers *et al.*, 2007, p263). The original Early Childhood Environmental Rating Scale (ECERS) (Harms *et al.*, 1998) was developed in the late 1980s in the USA as a tool to measure the effectiveness of the learning provision for young children, aged two to five years. It remains in widespread use in Early Years settings in the USA and the revised version (ECERS-R, Harms *et al.*, 2004) has increasingly carved a niche in the UK Early Years sector, *growing in reputation as a viable, rigorous and manageable* tool to evaluate quality (Mathers *et al.*, 2007, p263).

The key findings of the first stage of the longitudinal Effective Provision of Pre-School Education (EPPE) project (Sylva *et al.*, 2003) were noted in Chapter 2. In particular, these identified that the most effective adult interactions with children were those that occurred with qualified teachers. Later findings continue to concur with those from the pre-school period, and also indicate that good outcomes for children are linked to settings that do not prioritise either children's social or cognitive development but treat them as complementary (Sylva *et al.*, 2010). As early as 2004, Sylva and her team had identified the ECERS's potential in assessing effectiveness. However, they found that the original ECERS focused primarily on social outcomes and, following further research as part of the EPPE project, introduced a further scale – the Early Childhood Environment Rating Scale Extension (ECERS-E) – which includes criteria to assess cognitive achievement. Sylva *et al.* (2004) always intended that the two would be used in a complementary way. Papatheodorou (2004, p2) sees the real value of both these scales in their use *as a self-assessment and improvement tool* at setting level. As such, it has considerable potential for use by the EYP in assessing effectiveness.

The ECERS-R has seven sub-scales containing 43 items, which are rated on a seven-point scale; these are represented in Table 8.1.

Table 8.1 The Early Childhood Environmental Rating Scale – Revised

ECERS-R Items	ECERS-R sub-scales
1–8	Space and furnishings
9–14	Personal care routines
15–18	Language reasoning
19–28	Activities
29–33	Interaction
34–37	Programme structure
38–43	Parents and staff

Source: Sylva *et al.* (2010, p73)

The Early Years Environment Rating Scale Extension (ECERS-E) (Sylva *et al.*, 2003) was developed by members of the EPPE project team and contains an additional four sub-scales, consisting of 18 items, which are represented in Table 8.2. ECERS-E is more concerned with children's cognitive development.

Table 8.2 The Early Childhood Environmental Rating Scale – Extension

ECERS-E Items	ECERS-E sub-scales
1–6	Literacy
7–10	Mathematics
11–15	Science and environment
16–18	Diversity

Source: Sylva *et al.* (2010, p73)

The Early Years Quality Improvement Support Programme (EYQISP)

Linked to the outcomes of *Every Child Matters* (DfES, 2004) and the EYFS Principles (DCSF, 2008a), the Early Years Quality Improvement Support Programme (EYQISP) (DCSF, 2008c) has been introduced to provide tools for LA Early Years Consultants and the leaders of Early Years settings for supporting quality improvement. The focus in this programme takes the view that high-quality Early Years provision enhances children's long-term outcomes. Four main principles underpin the programme's tools:

1. the significant role of leadership in improving quality;

2. the role of the continuous cycle of self-evaluation, improvement and reflection;

3. a transparent system of challenge and support, agreed by everyone involved;

4. strong partnership established between the LA, the settings and their community.

These principles are then explored in the programme though five elements:

1. strengthening leadership for learning;

2. developing practitioner learning;

3. facilitating partnerships for learning and development;

4. supporting progress, learning and development;

5. securing high-quality environments for learning and development.

This programme acknowledges the complexity of quality improvement and that many factors contribute to high-quality Early Years provision. However, the programme provides a helpful visual model that summarises significant features of effective provision. These are grouped into three main areas: workforce, practice and environment. Appropriately, the child is placed at the centre of these areas (DCSF, 2008c, p9).

PRACTICAL TASK

The significant features of each area are represented in the tables below so that you can consider them against the EYP Standards. You can view the diagram in the programme handbook, which is referenced at the end of this chapter (DCSF, 2008c, p9).

Significant features of high-quality provision

Area 1: Practice	Relevant EYP Standards
Clear educational goals	
Meeting every child's needs	
Sustained shared thinking	
Warm responsive relationships between adults and children	
Parents supported in involvement in children's learning	

Area 2: Content and Environment	Relevant EYP Standards
EYFS staff:children ratios	
EYFS challenging and play-based content	
Safe and stimulating physical environment	

Area 3: Workforce	Relevant EYP Standards
Graduate leading practice, setting vision, leading learning culture	
Level 3 as standard for group care and basis for progression to higher levels	
CPD opportunities for staff to gain higher qualifications and improve skills	

Source: DCSF (2008c, p9)

REFLECTIVE TASK

- *How could these features complement the existing quality improvement measures in your setting?*

- *Identify any features that you would add to the areas above.*

There are other methods of measuring the effectiveness of children's learning. We considered the Effective Early Learning (EEL) project (Pascal and Bertram, 2000) in Chapter 6, along with the work of Ferre Laevers on children's involvement in their play (Laevers, 1994). These offer further insights into any review of early learning environments, and the EYFS makes reference to the use of both ECERS-R and the Leuven scale of children's well-being and involvement (Laevers, 1994) as quality improvement tools to ensure the continuous improvement of young children's provision (DCSF, 2008d, p9).

As an EYP, leading practice by example and in support of others, it is useful to consider the use of such formal assessment tools as those described above, which can provide a framework for evaluating all aspects of the provision for children's learning and development in your setting.

Self-assessment task

Having reflected on different aspects of the learning environment in the three sections above, you are encouraged to identify potential areas of development in your setting. In the middle column identify action you might take to address these areas. Finally, add any EYP Standards that are relevant to your proposed actions. You might find it helpful to refer back to the reflective task in Chapter 5, concerning the development of the environment (pages 78 and 79).

Identified areas for potential development	Proposed actions to address these areas of development	Related EYP Standards

Professional behaviour

In this chapter, we have seen that there are many factors to be considered when identifying, reviewing and developing high-quality provision in Early Years settings. However, the successful impact of the setting's provision on children's learning, development and well-being will also be largely dependent on the *level of dedication, commitment and effort of the people within it* (Siraj-Blatchford and Manni, 2007, p21). An EYP who has high expectations of everyone in the setting and models the behaviours they expect of others, will provide a positive role model for staff. They will seek ways to promote the development of all staff so they can contribute more effectively to the setting's delivery of high-quality practice. They will also consider how staff can contribute to the process of developing policy and practice that will impact on them directly. An EYP's open and respectful manner will help to engender the involvement and trust of others. EYPs will then be better placed to support and sustain *a culture of collaborative and co-operative working between colleagues* (S33) (CWDC, 2008, p64). This is explored more fully in the next and final chapter of the book.

Table 8.3 is the outcome of collaborative work by all members of a Children's Centre staff, who were involved in the development of a 'code of conduct', to be followed by everyone at the Centre. The staff decided which determining factors should be included in the code. These were: working to a high standard; respect; dedication; humour. There was then further discussion on how both the positive and negative qualities of each factor might be characterised.

Table 8.3 illustrates the agreed description of both positive and negative qualities of the four named factors, but the staff team identified 13 factors in total and the additional nine factors are listed below, though not exemplified.

Code of Conduct at a Children's Centre (2009), agreed by all staff members

1. *Excellent attendance*
2. *Respect for each other*
3. *Positive attitude*
4. *Supportive of colleagues*
5. *Courtesy*
6. *Well presented*
7. *Working to a high standard*
8. *Punctual*
9. *Dedication*
10. *Humour*
11. *Discretion*
12. *Flexibility*
13. *The children come first*

Table 8.3 Children's Centre 'Code of Conduct'

Working to a high standard	
Positive	**Negative**
Pulling your weight, being well prepared	Leaving work to others, being lazy
Effective communication	Lack of communication
Impact	**Impact**
Room routines flow and are effective	Resentment
Staff deployment excellent	High stress levels
Positive, calm environment	Increase in sickness
Fewer interruptions	Work doesn't get done
Children benefit	Staff feel left out, don't know what's going on
Consistency	

Respect	
Positive	**Negative**
Acknowledge each other's strengths	Not bothered to acknowledge everything
Respond to other people	Ignoring other people
Friendly atmosphere	Cold atmosphere
Impact:	**Impact:**
Staff self-esteem raised, better output	People become demoralised, demotivated
Using other people's strengths to support you	No communication
Welcoming atmosphere	Poor attendance
Brings the best out of people	Children affected by atmosphere
High morale	

Dedication	
Positive	**Negative**
Being prepared to give the extra inch	Not being prepared, winging it
Impact:	**Impact:**
Things get done	Resentment
Good positive atmosphere	Disruption
Can rely on each other	No respect
All help and support others	Abusing colleagues

Humour	
Positive	**Negative**
Seeing the funny side of things, being relaxed, Letting things that annoy you go sometimes	Taking everything too seriously
Impact:	**Impact:**
Laughter instead of offence	Continuous complaints to management
Laughter is contagious	Work time taken to resolve issues
People connect through humour	People being offended
	People feeling miserable
	People feeling lonely, not part of the group

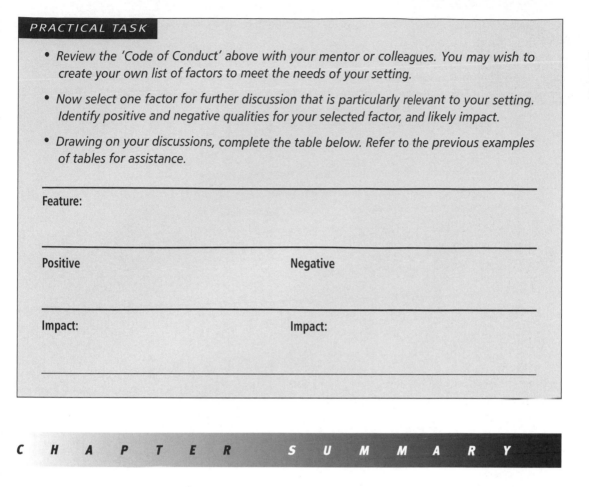

PRACTICAL TASK

- *Review the 'Code of Conduct' above with your mentor or colleagues. You may wish to create your own list of factors to meet the needs of your setting.*

- *Now select one factor for further discussion that is particularly relevant to your setting. Identify positive and negative qualities for your selected factor, and likely impact.*

- *Drawing on your discussions, complete the table below. Refer to the previous examples of tables for assistance.*

Feature:

Positive   **Negative**

Impact: **Impact:**

C H A P T E R   S U M M A R Y

This chapter has focused on the significance of high-quality Early Years provision and its influential impact on children's longer-term outcomes. We have examined a range of ways in which EYPs can raise the quality of practice in their settings in order to promote children's learning, development and well-being more effectively. We also examined the crucial role of parents in supporting their child's learning and development within the home environment. EYPs engage in respectful communication and establish positive relationships with parents in order to support them with this role. The case study material in this chapter revealed differing interpretations of quality indicators and you were encouraged to explore your own views on this subject. We finally considered how successful Early Years provision relies on staff working effectively together in order to support all children to reach their potential.

Moving on

In the final chapter of this book we focus on effective Early Years pedagogy and consider global influences on this subject. We will examine the topic of continuing professional development, as well as the supporting role of EYP Networks. We conclude this book by considering some opportunities to support and encourage future EYPs.

FURTHER READING

DCSF (2008c) *The Early Years Quality Improvement Support Programme*. Nottingham: DCSF.

Ofsted (n.d.) http://www.ofsted.gov.uk/ (accessed 12 February 2010).

Sylva, K, Melhuish, E, Sammons, P, Siraj-Blatchford, I and Taggart, B (2010) *Early Childhood Matters: Evidence from the Effective Pre-school and Primary Education Project* London: Routledge.

9 Continuing professional development

CHAPTER OBJECTIVES

This chapter draws together the key themes in the book, and looks ahead beyond the EYP assessment process to the ongoing role of the EYP and continuing professional development. Frameworks and ideologies for early learning beyond those in the English context are considered as it is believed these will further enhance the EYP's understanding of effective pedagogy and, in turn, support the quality of young children's learning. The establishment of EYP Networks (EYPN) across England is appraised and further opportunities for professional development through the EYPN and beyond are considered.

After reading this chapter you should be able to:
- critically appraise models of early learning from the Reggio Emilia pre-schools in Italy, *Te Whāriki* approach to Early Learning in New Zealand, Forest Schools in Denmark and High Scope in the USA;
- reflect on the professional development opportunities that Early Years Professional Status offers;
- demonstrate understanding of the place of the EYP Networks in offering post-validation support and ongoing opportunities for study and learning.

While also presenting a synoptic view of the themes addressed in the book relating to Early Years pedagogy, the focus of this chapter is on the EYP's ongoing professional development. As such it has broad relevance to many of the Standards for Early Years Professionals, particularly 38 and 39.

Introduction

Effective pedagogy

The overarching aim of this book has been to enable the EYP to gain a deeper understanding of Early Years pedagogy and how the EYP role is key to enhancing the effectiveness of practice within the EYFS and improving outcomes for children. We have considered aspects of theory and key research studies that inform contemporary understanding, and set these in the practical context of planning for children's learning and development within an enabling environment. There has been considerable emphasis on the role of the EYP – the pedagogue – in children's learning, ensuring an inclusive approach that enables and facilitates learning for every child. The concept of sustained shared thinking, so central to the EYP role and clearly embedded within the EYFS principles and themes (DCSF, 2008e), has been addressed, and quality indicators of effective practice discussed. In this final chapter, we offer further reflections on the significance of the EYP role in the development of the Children's Workforce, and focus on post-validation and the importance of a commitment to *continuing a personal and professional learning journey*.

Any history of the role of the Early Years practitioner would show a separation of those who *care* for babies and young children and those who *educate* them. The legacy of such a separation has been what McGillivray (2008, p245) describes as a *dichotomy between a workforce that is construed as caring, maternal, gendered, as opposed to professional, degree educated and highly trained*, and this has been reflected in the range of titles given to the roles of the Early Years practitioner. McGillivray (2008) suggests that such breadth in nomenclature has contributed to the uncertainty of public perception of the Early Years workforce. With the advent of the role of Early Years Professional (CWDC, 2009a), we are seeing a gradual public shift in understanding of the professionalism that is now both explicitly and implicitly stated within this new role and within Early Years practice and provision generally. As we noted in Chapter 1, as an EYP you have a key role to play here in shaping such constructs and perceptions of this professionalism – both within the workforce and in wider society. This is not without its significant challenges, and the following case studies show how three EYPs are experiencing this.

CASE STUDY

Claire, EYP and manager of a private nursery

I am passionate about the new professionalism that is part of the Children's Workforce now. Although I am the manager of the setting and am officially 'supernumerary', since achieving EYPS, the company has recognised the importance of my status and I now spend significant blocks of time each week in the different base rooms in the nursery so I can lead by example and work directly with staff and children in implementing key changes to practice. This is what I want to, and believe I should, be doing.

CASE STUDY

Elizabeth, followed the full-pathway route to EYPS following a career change from her previous role as a secondary school teacher

The full-pathway route has been both exciting and hugely challenging but I am finding my confidence is growing through the opportunities I have to lead others' practice both indoors and outdoors. At first, I met some resistance from other staff but my mentor and the room leader where I am placed have been very supportive and very co-operative – and they are both increasingly willing to allow me to take on the role of lead practitioner. My work on behaviour management and on using drama to support learning in the pre-

CASE STUDY continued

school are both areas that they wish to continue after my placement at the nursery has finished. It is really encouraging that they recognise the importance of the EYP role for the workforce.

CASE STUDY

Nancy, EYP and a childminder

While I still find some colleagues in my local Childminding Network questioning the point of gaining additional qualifications and achieving EYPS, a lot of my colleagues now value the experience and knowledge I have, and frequently consult me about practice issues. I believe I am exercising leadership in doing so and try to inspire them. Certainly, the parents of my children have been very supportive of my achieving EYPS .

REFLECTIVE TASK

You can see in the above case studies a mixture of opportunity and challenge in the EYP role, especially with colleagues. What have been the issues you have faced so far in seeking to contribute to the professionalisation of the Early Years workforce through your progress to EYPS?

Global influences on Early Years pedagogy

Petrie (2005, p293) reminds us that 'globalisation' is very much in our midst with the multicultural context in which we live and work, with *migration affecting how we see ourselves in relation to the rest of the social world and to the physical environment*. The implications of this are two-fold: first, as we discussed in Chapter 3, we must take seriously the socio-cultural context in which we work and, for the EYP, it is particularly important to reflect on how this influences your own pedagogical base; second, we remain open to learning from the ways other nations 'do' Early Years practice, and reflect on how this might impact on our work.

We now turn to a range of approaches and perspectives that have already influenced contemporary understanding of Early Years pedagogy and, indeed, are continuing to do so. There is a wide range of literature available that offers more in-depth understanding of these, and, indeed, within this series, Palaiologou (2008) has already made significant reference to the approaches from Italy (Reggio Emilia) and New Zealand (*Te Whāriki*). Many find these different perspectives to be fresh, exciting, innovative and inspiring, though most of the principles on which they have been developed are not, in fact, new but – rather – rooted in the theories of the reformers we discussed in Chapter 2. The difference here is in the *complete package(s) of ideas and the way they are put into practice* (Johnston and Nahmad-Williams, 2009, p36). However, caution is necessary lest we try to *borrow another identity* (Papatheodorou, 2004) without fully taking into account our own socio-cultural context. Pere (1983, p1) reminds us that *learning is always part of one's own life experiences and learning in the formative years is particularly subject to culturally ascribed values*. Thus, in any appraisal of approaches used in cultural contexts other than our own, a spirit of critical reflection is required (Standards 38 and 39).

Reggio Emilia pre-schools

Quite deliberately, this approach is considered first because – perhaps above all other international perspectives – it has been the catalyst for significant reflection on provision and practice in Early Years settings in England, not least through the influential 'Hundred Languages of Children' exhibition that toured the UK in the 1990s. Indeed, the title of the exhibition was inspired by a poem by Loris Malaguzzi, a trained primary school teacher and founder of the Reggio Emilia pre-schools, in which he sets out the fundamental pedagogical principle of the Reggio Approach: that children have a whole range – *a hundred languages . . . and a hundred more . . .* (Malguzzi, cited in Fillipini and Vecchi, 1997, p3) – of ways of interpreting their experiences and of representing their ideas about the world. The municipal pre-schools of Reggio Emilia in northern Italy, led by Malaguzzi, came into existence in 1963, with their origins very clearly rooted in the commitment of the local community that children of this and subsequent generations *would never again . . . tolerate injustice and inequality* such as that shown up to and during the Second World War (Thornton and Brunton, 2009, p9).

What is fresh in the Reggio approach is the interpretation of inherited theoretical and philosophical understanding of young children and early childhood, and how this has been *articulated into a coherent pedagogical praxis* (Papatheodorou, 2006, p2). Malaguzzi's vision was of a pedagogy that sees learning as a shared relational experience involving child, parents, educators and the local community. The fundamental principles of the Reggio approach are seen in:

- *the image of the child* – *as rich in potential, strong, powerful, competent and – most of all – connected to adults and other children* (Malaguzzi, 1993, p10);

- *the approach to the curriculum (progetazzione)* – the concept here is of an emergent model that originates from the children's ideas and interests, and that is then developed by the educators into a project, short- or long-term, which itself evolves as the children ask new questions and discover new problems to solve;

- *the role of the educator* – in each of the pre-school rooms there are two qualified Early Years teachers supported by a range of assistants; in most of the pre-schools there is also a setting-based *atelierista*, trained in the visual arts, who provides specialised support as the children seek to develop their own representative expression of their ideas in art work; the role of the adult in the Reggio approach is seen as observing, listening to and 'partnering' their learning;

- *the parental role* – parents are viewed as their children's first, and principal, 'teacher', and their contribution within and beyond the classrooms is respected and valued highly; many of the ideas for the emergent curriculum are developed from conversations with parents and children;

- *the learning environment* – viewed as the 'third educator' with very careful thought given to its design; teachers, together with the *atelierista* seek to capitalise on natural light and maximise the use of natural materials, such as plants and seeds; a rich supply of resources is attractively presented to encourage the children to explore and express themselves, especially through representational artwork, which is then displayed throughout the setting.

Self-assessment task

Using some of the Principles into Practice (PiP) Cards from the EYFS Pack (DCSF, 2008e), can you see the influence of the Reggio approach on the pedagogy promoted in the EYFS? Try to identify an example from your own practice to illustrate this. Note your ideas in the table below.

PiP Card	Link with the Reggio approach	Example from own practice
1.1 A Unique Child		
2.2 Parents as Partners		
2.3 Supporting Learning		
3.1 Observation, Assessment and Planning		
3.3 The Learning Environment		
4.2 Active Learning		

Te Whāriki

As long ago as 1986, New Zealand became the first country in the world to combine the national administration of Early Years care services with pre-school education (Moss 2000) and, in its ten-year strategic plan (New Zealand Ministry of Education (NZME), 2002), early education is presented as a *multi-disciplinary field that draws on knowledge from diverse areas* (Dalli, 2008, p173). Nowhere is this exemplified more effectively than in *Te Whāriki* (NZME, 1996), New Zealand's curriculum framework for early learning, which draws on the Maori word for 'weaving' – *whāriki* – to illustrate that children's early learning is not in discrete subject or learning areas but rather arises *when professionally trained [adults], soundly grounded in the . . . specialist knowledge bases of child development and early childhood [theory] draw knowledgeably on other disciplines and work collaboratively with other professionals . . .* (Dalli, 2008, p173).

Te Whāriki itself is founded on several principles that merge into an approach based on children's interests. It is an aspirational framework for learning, which seeks to use a bicultural paradigm (Maori and Western European), encouraging *the transmission of* my *cultural values,* my *language and* customs – *with your cultural values, language and customs. It validates my belief systems and your belief systems also* . . . (Reedy, 1995, p17, cited in Pakai, 2004, p1). Fundamentally, *Te Whāriki* is about providing children with a strong base that teaches respect for self and others, with a strong belief that this crosses cultures and can ultimately weave people and nations together (Pakai, 2004). The principles that underpin the framework are as follows.

* *Empowerment (Whakamana)* – the fundamental aim of the framework is that it empowers the child's learning and development.

* *Holistic development (Kotahitanga)* – recognising the whole child and taking full account of their world, acknowledging the interconnectedness of social, cultural, physical, emotional and spiritual aspects of development.

* *Family and community (Whanau Tangata)* – acknowledging that the child's wider world of family and community are core to their experience of childhood.

* *Relationships (Nga Hononga)* – drawing strongly on theories about the social and interactional nature of learning (based on Bandura, 1977; Vygotsky and Cole, 1978).

Pre-schools have the freedom to create and develop their own programmes within *Te Whāriki's* common framework of principles – acknowledging that each setting has its own unique context, with each child's cultural background, home language and interests a core part of this development.

PRACTICAL TASK

Think of the 'principled approach' embedded within the EYFS (DCSF, 2008d) and see how close this is to Te Whāriki *principles. From plans for the programme in your setting and/or entries in children's profiles/learning journeys, are you also able to identify a specific example of how these principles are demonstrated in practice? Note your ideas in the table below. You might like to discuss with a colleague how these link to the EYP Standards.*

EYFS theme	*Te Whāriki* principle	Example from practice (linked to programme plans/children's profiles)	Link to EYP Standards
A Unique Child			
Positive Relationships			
Enabling Environment			
Learning and Development			

Forest Schools

Although the original concept for Forest School came from Sweden in the 1950s, it was not until the 1980s in Denmark that it became established as an educational method in its own right for pre-school children (under seven years), stemming from the Danish *småbørnspaedogik* (can you see that word 'pedagogy' again here?), the approach to Early Years education (Archimedes Training, 2009). It is an approach that has grown rapidly in many parts of the world, including the UK, since the 1990s. Forest Schools use natural areas of woodland and forests to provide a safe outdoor environment through which children can learn by exploration, embedded in a secure routine that is established early in the programme. What distinguishes Forest Schools from a typical outdoor learning environment attached to a setting is the freedom children have to explore the ever-changing environment and to *assess and take risks for themselves* (Lindon, 1999, p10). In addition to learning informally and at first hand about nature and natural processes, which proponents of the approach describe as *touching something deep within the child* (Weaver, 1998, cited in Massey, 2005, p1), the Scandinavian Forest School approach offers children the opportunity to build on skills from week to week at their own pace, with play, creativity, socialisation and emotional stability at its centre (Knight, 2009).

Fundamental to the Forest School approach is that it is led by the child's interests, within a *loose skills framework with supportive intervention by qualified leaders* (Massey, 2005, p1). All aspects of learning are incorporated in the Forest School approach and *by following what children point out first . . . [the adult] can set challenges* (Grenier, 1999, p13) so that all the senses are stimulated, the children's imagination captured and their understanding of their environment set in a real context. Studies (such as Dillon *et al.*, 2006) suggest that children in Forest Schools have higher levels of well-being than their urban peers, have fewer days off sick, are better able to concentrate and have more advanced skills of physical co-ordination. As a consequence, for such children, transition into school becomes a more positive experience, with their demonstrating stronger social skills, greater ability to work in groups and with higher levels of self confidence than non-Forest School peers.

Knight (2009, p5) believes that the growth of Forest Schools in the UK is symbolic of the successful *transformation of an idea from one culture to another*. An increasing number of Early Years settings are now aiming to implement aspects of the approach into their pedagogy, with regular trips to a local woodland area for the three- to five-year-old age group. Typically such visits follow the same basic format so the children become familiar with it and know what to expect. Sessions include 'talking time' to brief the children about safety, to recall the previous session's activities and introduce them to the day. On their way into the forest, the children talk about anything that interests them and, once arrived at the site, they sing a familiar Forest School song, before hand washing, snack and story time. The children then have a minimum of one hour for free exploration of/play in the Forest School area, hunting for mini-beasts, gathering leaves, making dens, and so on. Before leaving, the children have the opportunity to review and share what they have been doing, and all are encouraged to take back an item they have found, made or created in the forest, or to take a digital photograph if this is not possible. En route back to their own setting, they sing the Forest School song again.

Regular visits to woodland areas are not practicable for all settings, but the following case study shows how one EYP, Menna, has been able to apply Forest School principles to her own practice. She had the opportunity to visit Early Years settings in Denmark as part of a study trip with her EYPS training provider. She had always believed strongly in the importance of outdoor learning and there is a well-established in/out flow to the provision she offers in her nursery.

CASE STUDY

Menna, EYP and manager of a pre-school offering sessional care

Since achieving EYPS, I have been able to take part in an EYP Network study trip to some Forest Schools in Denmark. I have been able to draw on this rich opportunity in my practice. We do take our children out into woodland areas when we can and, recently, my setting successfully bid for a capital access grant to redevelop the garden. I spent time discussing with the children, parents and staff how to spend the money. We used large sheets of paper with small groups of children to let them draw their ideas for the design of the garden, and asked individual children to walk me round the existing garden (a field of mud!) and explain what they would like to have in the new one. I was able to video these walks. All the children wanted to keep puddles and mud in the new design. I have tried to draw on many of the ideas from Forest School thinking about the outdoor space, including the principle that 'less is more'. I was able to use the ideas gathered from the above research to design the new garden. We have laid some grass and incorporated a small hill, and are now about to plant a willow structure to create some 'hiding places'. I have encouraged staff to hide a range of artefacts in the sandpit for the children to 'discover', and we have areas for children to dig and plant, as well as access to water play.

REFLECTIVE TASK

The significance of the outdoors in early learning is well documented (e.g. Bilton, 2002; Ouvry, 2003; Tovey, 2007) and was addressed in Chapter 5. Think how Forest School principles enhance evidence of the importance of outdoor learning and consider how you might apply these principles to provision in your setting.

High Scope

The final international perspective considered here (and you are strongly encouraged to broaden your understanding of Early Years pedagogy by researching others) is the High Scope Approach. This was originally developed in 1962 by David Weikart, a psychologist in Yspilanti, Michigan, in the United States, to *serve at-risk children from poor neighbourhoods* (Cahir, 2008, p3), with its goal to improve the intellectual, social and emotional learning and development of such children, and thus improve their later educational and life experiences. High Scope is the only one of the four covered here that has been the subject of internal and independent longitudinal evaluation for 40 years and more (e.g. Schweinhart, 2000). Such evaluative studies suggest that adolescents and adults who, as children, had been introduced to the High Scope approach within pre-school settings, show increased social responsibility, enhanced chance of higher economic status, improved educational performance, and increased capacity to make and maintain long-term relationships (High Scope Educational Research Foundation, 2007). Having earlier considered the EPPE project (Sylva *et al.*, 2003) we can see that its aims – likewise – are to monitor outcomes for children over time and should yield valuable data.

High Scope offers a framework for learning that is underpinned by the belief that children learn best from activities planned and carried out by themselves in partnership with adults in a cycle of *plan–do–review* (Hohmann and Weikart, 2002). It is based on sound educational principles and, once again, you will note the commonality between these principles and those of the approaches already considered and, indeed, of our own EYFS (DCSF, 2008d).

- *Active learning* – children need first-hand experiences through actively engaging with people, materials, events and ideas that are meaningful to them.

- *Personal initiative* – children have a natural drive to learn, and should be allowed autonomy and independence to plan and develop their own plans and interests. Thus, they are encouraged to select their own learning programme (*plan*), generate their own learning experiences (*do*) and then to reflect on those (*review*).

- *Consistency* – the High Scope approach provides secure routines, relationships and organisation within which effective learning can take place.

- *Genuine relationships* – practitioners aim to bring genuine care, warmth and trust to the children, and show respect for each child's personal and cultural identity.

- *Appropriate curriculum* – the framework for learning has been developed through extensive observations of young children, based on developmental indicators that provide children with the foundation of knowledge, skills and ideas so vital to later life.

Source: adapted from High Scope Educational Research Foundation (2007)

In the following case study, an EYP describes how she is embedding some of the High Scope principles into her practice.

CASE STUDY

Kaniza, an EYP who leads the pre-school room in a Children's Centre

Kaniza leads the pre-school room in a Children's Centre set in an area of high unemployment, high crime levels and community disharmony. As part of her own programme of study for EYPS, Kaniza learned about the High Scope approach and its principles in a setting similar to her own, and explored how she might adapt this in her own practice.

First of all, I had to convince the staff team. Many were sceptical but I was convinced of the value of continuing with this so I persisted as gently as I could and, at a staff meeting

---

CASE STUDY continued

we were having, I managed to secure some video evidence from High Scope UK and that was the push the team needed. We do now use the plan–do–review approach, using daily sheets with visual symbols of activities that children can tick or circle to show their choices. We make sure that the menu of options (a) is based on the children's current interests and (b) offers them breadth and balance within the EYFS Framework. We have a system of reviewing the programme with individual children when we can but then structure in time with our key groups at the end of each session, reviewing with the children what they have been doing. We've only been using this approach for about six months but already we can see that all our children are more motivated and in control of their own learning.

REFLECTIVE TASK

Can you see links between the High Scope approach – especially in how Kaniza has applied this to her practice – and Standards 7, 8, 10, 11, 13, 22 and 27?

Building a community of learners

Reflection on models and approaches to early learning beyond those familiar to you is one indicator that, as an EYP, you are committed to effective practice. Beyond this, you are also challenged to role model yourself as a 'good learner' to colleagues, children and parents. Siraj-Blatchford and Manni (2007) identify the characteristics or patterns of leadership that can be seen in settings judged to be offering the highest-quality early learning experiences for children and families. Their study defines one important aspect of the leadership role to be that of *building a learning community and team culture* (Siraj-Blatchford and Manni, 2007, p21). In demonstrating your own commitment to ongoing learning and development, you are encouraging colleagues to do likewise. The wealth of knowledge, understanding and skills developed and acquired already about Early Years practice and provision is huge but there is still so much more to learn. It's a truism that, the more we know, the more we realise we do *not* know, and this clearly applies to our knowledge about young children and how they learn and develop. Although your immediate goal is to achieve EYPS, you can also begin to think about opportunities for further learning. Many EYPs continue on to further study on relevant short postgraduate courses, or explore opportunities for progression to awards at full master's level.

As can be seen in the following case studies, EYPs represent a wide range of backgrounds and experience – and, indeed, there is no such person as a 'typical EYP' – but common ground is found when each takes the opportunity to reflect on their own learning and to identify appropriate, and often innovative, ways of supporting the effective practice of others.

CASE STUDY

Clare, a Children's Centre teacher and Early Years consultant, approaching EYPS validation

Even though I have had a full and varied career as a teacher in many Early Years settings, I am learning so much from my current baby room experience about very early development and learning, and about how to lead practice from 'within' the setting by sharing with colleagues what I myself am learning.

CASE STUDY

Becky, at the point of EYPS validation and assistant manager at a Children's Centre

I have worked my way up from a level 3 NVQ and am now in Year 3 of a BA Childhood Studies degree. My studies have given me opportunity to gain an insight into the theory of practice – why children, and adults for that matter, do certain things at certain times in certain ways. I believe I now reflect in depth on why I 'do' practice like I do, and seek to monitor ways I can improve my own practice. Also, through my studies, I have gained confidence in my own ability and can now stand up for what I believe is 'best practice', sharing this with colleagues, to ensure that children within our centre have the best start in life.

CASE STUDY

Pam, EYP and a childminder

Within my Childminding Network is a colleague who has been childminding for 30 years, and when I first began the pathway towards EYPS, I felt that it would be completely inappropriate for me to try to offer help and advice to someone so experienced (notions of 'grandmother' and 'sucking eggs' rang bells). However, through my own studies, my confidence has grown – as has my commitment to high-quality childminding – and I do now feel able to offer my judgement if she asks my advice. For instance, recently we were both observing the 18 month old she looks after. The other childminder mentioned that the child liked nothing better than putting things into boxes and then tipping them out again. I was able to talk about the place of schemas in development and give her some advice about the type of activities she could offer the child to support her learning at this time. The other childminder was really interested to learn about this.

Claire, EYP and manager of a private nursery

Since achieving EYPS, I have developed new planning and profile formats – introducing them to staff and parents – and reviewed the layout, organisation and resources of each of our rooms. But I think more important than this 'doing' has been the realisation that I now reflect much more on all that I do. And I listen to my staff a lot more. I think, having the confidence from my own studies and EYPS preparation, I now believe I am implementing the right changes into the setting and am able to explain why I am doing certain things.

Rachel, a full-pathway EYPS candidate, at point of validation in an under-threes setting

It's been a rollercoaster of a year and so challenging in so many ways but I can't wait now to start my new job [leader of a sessional pre-school setting] and know I have the confidence to take responsibility for leading practice on a more long-term basis than has been possible on the full-pathway route. That said, I feel that I am now an effective practitioner in the toddler room. I can use the knowledge I have acquired over the last year to influence change and to offer challenges for the children. I have a good working relationship with the team leader in the room and I have worked well with her. She has the self-confidence and desire to succeed and do the best by the children so is happy to ask for advice or to bat ideas off me to get the result she wants. I have supported her with baking, heuristic play and implementing aspects of the Mosaic Approach.

Although from very different settings and backgrounds, each of the EYPs in the above case studies describes a growing confidence in her own learning, and articulates a change in professional identity that has emerged from development of her knowledge and skills.

- *Are you able to reflect on how your confidence as a learner and your own professional identity have grown as you move towards EYPS?*

- *Can you think of specific examples of how you demonstrate this?*

- *What and/or who has enabled you so far?*

- *Are you able to begin to identify the next steps on your own learning journey once you have achieved EYPS?*

Early Years Professional Networks

While the achievement of EYPS is rightly to be celebrated, it can be viewed as a 'beginning' rather than an 'ending'. As the number of Early Years Professionals has grown, EYP Networks have now become established in most local authorities. These will be evolving differently in each area, according to the needs, aspirations and motivations of a particular group of EYPs, but Brodie (2008) outlines how all are seen as key to offering opportunities to expand professional expertise. Several Networks offer monthly meetings, which are organised round specific training requirements, such as schematic development. A number of benefits have been identified by members, which include: continued professional development; sharing with and learning from peers within the group; visits to other settings; information about further study; and a shared sense of professional identity within this community of practice.

Look at the following two case studies, which illustrate the potential benefits of EYP Networks for both the EYP and the local authority.

CASE STUDY

Milissa, an EYP and deputy manager in a private nursery

I became involved with the local EYP Network at its outset, when we were brought together by the local authority. Our first task was to determine the purpose of the Network, apart from a vehicle for sharing good practice. We were from a variety of different Early Years settings, with a wealth of experience and different agendas. After much discussion, we felt that the best way forward was to take on a research project with funding available from the CWDC. We opted for the area of outdoor play as this was a very topical subject both nationally and in our local area, and we wanted to investigate how we could help improve the provision for outdoor play in local settings. In order to help gain practical knowledge and inspiration as to how we can develop this area in our own practice, we planned a series of visits to inspirational settings both here and in Europe. The project culminated in the presentation of our findings, along with the changes our research had brought about in our own settings, at a conference attended by other Early Years settings in the area. We are now in the process of change – deciding in what direction the Network will go.

The CWDC describes one of the roles of Early Years Professionals as to lead and support other staff by helping them to develop and improve their practice. I feel my involvement in the Network has helped me to fulfil this duty by sharing good practice with the other members and hopefully by sharing our research with other settings in the local area. It has also had a big impact on my own professional development. I have been pushed way out of my comfort zone of working in the same familiar setting on a daily basis, as I have been asked to attend various local and national events to speak about my experiences. It has given me the confidence to recognise my own achievements, and how to best lead and motivate my colleagues to recognise theirs.

A local authority Children's Workforce manager

From a local authority's perspective, it is important to have an EYP Network to provide those newly awarded the status with a group of fellow-professionals with whom they can identify and not feel isolated. The Network is seen as a key forum for consultation, where common goals can be built upon and appropriate workshops offered. Crucially, it is a forum for dissemination of good practice, and a safe place where issues round the role in the workplace can be identified and addressed. More long term, the Network is a place where EYPs have the opportunity to research and develop areas of expertise, which they can then cascade to colleagues. If used appropriately, local authorities believe the Network offers key opportunities for personal and professional development beyond EYPS.

Inspiring others

It is fitting that we conclude this book with the notion of the 'full circle'. As you reflect back on your own route to EYPS, and your own personal and professional learning journey to this point, it is important also to look ahead to the next generation of EYPs and your role in encouraging and supporting them. Many EYPs become mentors, tutors and assessors within the EYPS process and, as such, bring a welcome authenticity and shared understanding to this work. You might like to reflect on how you are modelling the role of EYP, and think about how you can play your part in identifying and supporting future leaders of practice. See how Sandra, in the following case study, has built on her own experiences as an EYP here and is developing her capacity to support new EYPs at the same time as continuing with study for herself.

Sandra, EYP and manager of a private nursery

Since achieving EYPS, I feel that one of the biggest contributions I have brought to children's learning is the perspective I have from my own study visit to Denmark with my EYPS training provider. I have always aimed to see the 'whole' child and to develop the child's interests and ideas, and now believe I use the outdoor learning opportunities much more effectively – enabling the children in my setting to have a Forest School experience – even without a real forest! I have been able to share my reflections with a number of classes of Childhood Studies students at the nearby university – through presentations and discussions, inspiring them, hopefully, to understand the role of pedagogue and the Danish philosophy that is exemplified in the Forest School approach.

I now work as an EYPS mentor, tutor and assessor, and believe that my own continuing role as a lead practitioner, together with having undergone the same EYPS preparation and assessment process myself, enables me to fulfil these roles effectively. I have also

---

CASE STUDY *continued*

commenced study for an MA. My group is a mix of Early Years [school] teachers and Early Years Professionals, which makes for a dynamic all of its own as we bounce ideas off each other.

C H A P T E R   S U M M A R Y

In this final chapter, we have focused on the future: your role post-validation, and the opportunities that are open to you to continue to develop personally and professionally. In particular, we have reflected on the possibilities to develop and enhance practice by drawing on insights from different pedagogical models of early learning than those most familiar to us in the UK. We then discussed the importance not only of continuing to access further learning opportunities for yourselves, through study at master's level and other accredited higher education programmes, but also of sharing your knowledge and understanding appropriately with colleagues in order to best support effective practice across your setting. The key role of EYP Networks, and the opportunities these offer for mutual support, for disseminating good practice and as a discussion forum, have been outlined.

Fundamentally, we have aimed to describe and illustrate the need for a pedagogy that is not simply focused on the practice of teaching but is about reflection and theorising; it is about weaving the conceptual/theorising with the practical and interactional elements of teaching and learning so that EYPs can respond effectively to children's strengths and interests (Moyles *et al.*, 2002). We trust that this book has enabled and empowered you to establish a firm pedagogical base for your own practice, and the way you support, lead and inspire the practice of others.

FURTHER READING

You can read more about the models and approaches to Early Years practice outlined in this chapter at:

*   Reggio Emilia – www.reggioemiliaapproach.net

*   *Te Whāriki* – www.educate.ece.govt.nz

*   Forest School – www.forestschools.com

*   High Scope – www.high-scope.org.uk/about_highscope/18.asp

Additional recommended reading is as follows.

Davis, B (2004) International perspectives on Early Years education and care (Part 2, Chapter 7), in Willan, J, Parker-Rees, R and Savage, J (eds) *Early Childhood Studies.* Exeter: Learning Matters.

Paige-Smith, A and Craft, A (2008) Reflection and developing a community of practice (Part 3, Chapter 11), in Paige-Smith, A and Craft, A (eds) *Developing Reflective Practice in the Early Years.* Maidenhead: Open University Press/McGraw-Hill Education.

Appendix 1:
Piaget's stages of
cognitive development

Stage	Characteristics
Sensori-motor (birth to 2 years)	Reflexive movements in response to stimuli, which lead to development of early 'ideas'; young child recognises self as 'agent of action' and begins to act intentionally; achieves object permanence
Pre-operational (2 to 7 years)	Learns to use language meaningfully; can represent objects through images and words; thinking is developing but still egocentric, uncoordinated and 'irrational'; can classify objects by a single feature
Concrete operational (7 to 11 years)	Can think logically about objects and events; achieves 'conservation of number'; can classify according to several features; child still needs to think and operate concretely – with real objects, etc.
Formal operational (11+ years)	Can think logically about abstract concepts and ideas, and test hypotheses systematically; children are able to solve problems mentally

Source: adapted from Atherton (2009)

Appendix 2: Further Piagetian concepts

Schema (or scheme)	The representation in the mind of a set of perceptions, ideas and/or actions that link together; schemas are categories of knowledge that help young children make sense of the world; this work has been developed effectively by Athey (2007)
Schematic development	Observable patterns of behaviour in young children, which stem from their preoccupations and interests; Early Years practitioners use insights from observations and assessments of children's schematic development to enable them to see the uniqueness of each child's learning, and to provide possible lines of development for planning the programme
Assimilation	The process by which an individual takes information into their mind from their environment and/or experience, which may involve changing 'previously held information' to make sense of new ideas
Accommodation	The difference made to one's thinking through the process of assimilation; assimilation and accommodation are inextricably linked
Equilibration	All children strive for a balance between assimilation and accommodation; this process is called equilibration; as children progress through the stages of cognitive development, a balance between applying previous knowledge (assimilation) and changing behaviour/understanding to account for new knowledge (accommodation) needs to be maintained

Source: adapted from Atherton (2009)

References

Abbott, L and Rodger, R (2003) *Quality Education in the Early Years*. Buckingham: Open University Press.

Ainsworth, MDS and Bell, SM (1970) Attachment, exploration and separation: illustrated by the behaviour of one year olds in a strange situation. *Child Development*, March, 41: 49–67.

Anning, A and Edwards, A (2010) Young children as learners, in Miller, L, Cable, C and Goodliff, G (eds) *Supporting Children's Learning in the Early Years* (2nd edn). London: Routledge.

Applebee, AN and Langer, JA (1983) Instructional scaffolding: reading and writing as natural learning activities. *Language Arts*, 60(2): 168–175.

Archimedes Training (2009) *A History of Forest Schools*. Available online at: www.forestschools.com/history-of-forest-schools.php (accessed 5 January 2010).

Atherton, JS (2009) *Learning and Teaching: Piaget's Development Theory*. Available online at: www.learningandteaching.info/learning/piaget.htm (accessed 7 December 2009).

Athey, C (1990) *Extending Thought in Young Children: A Parent–Teacher Partnership*. London: Paul Chapman Publishing.

Athey, C (2007) *Extending Thought in Young Children: A Parent–Teacher Partnership* (2nd edn). London: Paul Chapman.

Bain, A and Barnett, L (1986) *The Design of a Day Care System in a Nursery Setting for Children Under Five: An Abridged Version of a Report of an Action Research Project*. Document No. 2T347. London: Tavistock Institute of Human Relations.

Ball, C (1994) *Start Right: The Importance of Early Learning*. London: Royal Society of Arts.

Bandura, A (1973) *Aggression: A Social Learning Analysis*. Englewood Cliffs, NJ: Prentice-Hall.

Bandura, A (1977) *Social Learning Theory*. London: Prentice Hall.

Bee, H and Boyd, D (2007) *The Developing Child*. New York: Pearson Education.

Bilton, H (2002) *Outdoor Play in the Early Years: Management and Innovation*. London: David Fulton.

Bottle, G (2007) Leadership in the Early Years, in Nurse, A (ed.) *The New Early Years Professional: Dilemmas and Debates*. London: Routledge.

Bowlby, J (1958) The nature of a child's tie to his mother. *International Journal of Psychoanalysis*, 39: 350–373.

Bowlby, J (1960a) Separation anxiety: a critical review of the literature. *Journal of Child Psychology and Psychiatry*, 1: 251–269.

Bowlby, J (1960b) Grief and mourning in infancy and early childhood. *The Psychoanalytic Study of Children*, 39: 350–373.

Bowlby, J (1988) *A Secure Base: Clinical Applications of Attachment Theory*. London: Routledge.

British Educational Research Association Early Years Special Interest Group (2003) *Early Years Research: Pedagogy, Curriculum and Adult Roles, Training and Professionalism*. Available online at: www.bera.ac.uk/files/reviews/beraearlyyearsreview31may03.pdf (accessed 2 December 2009).

Broadhead, P (2004) *Early Years Play and Learning: Developing Social Skills and Cooperation*. London: Routledge.

Broadhead, P (2008) Conflict and risk-taking in play: bridging home–school cultures. Play Colloquium paper, Leeds: LMU.

Broadhead, P, Howard, J and Wood, E (2010) *Play and Learning in Early Childhood Settings – Theory and Practice*. London: Sage.

Brodie, K (2008) What is the purpose of an EYP Network? *Nursery World*, 30 October: 23.

Bronfenbrenner, U (1979) *The Ecology of Human Development*. Cambridge, MA: Harvard University Press.

Brooker, L (2008) *Supporting Transitions in the Early Years*. Maidenhead: OUP.

Brown, B (1998) *Unlearning Discrimination in the Early Years*. Stoke-on-Trent: Trentham Books.

Browne, NW (2007) *The World in which We Occur: John Dewey, Pragmatist Ecology and American Ecological Writing in the 20th Century*. Tuscaloosa, AL: University of Alabama Press.

Bruner, J (1961) The act of discovery. *Harvard Educational Review*, 31: 21–32.

Bruner, J (1966) *Studies in Cognitive Growth: A Collaboration at the Centre for Cognitive Studies*. New York: Wiley & Son.

Bruner, J (1978) The role of dialogue in language acquisition, in Sinclair, A, Jarvelle, RJ and Levelt, WJM (eds) *The Child's Concept of Language*. New York: Springer-Verlag.

Cabinet Office (2009) *New Opportunities: Fair Chances for the Future*. Norwich: The Stationery Office.

Cahir, P (2008) *High Scope Program Briefing Paper*. Submitted to the Department for Education Employment and Workplace Relations by Early Childhood Australia Inc., September. Available online at: www.earlychildhoodaustralia.org.au/pdf/papers/ecahighscope.pdf (accessed 4 January 2010).

Cameron, C (2006) *New Ways of Educating: Pedagogy and Children's Services*. London: Thomas Coram Research Unit/Institute of Education, University of London.

Carr, M (2001) *Assessment in Early Childhood Settings*. London: Sage.

Children's Workforce Development Council (CWDC) (2005) *Children's Workforce Strategy: A Consultation*. Nottingham: Department for Education and Skills.

CWDC (2008) *Guidance to the Standards for the Award of Early Years Professional Status* (revised). Leeds: CWDC.

CWDC (2009a) *Early Years Professional Status: What does an EYP do?* London: CWDC. Available online at: www.cwdcouncil.org.uk/about/faq#Q_414 (accessed 25 October 2009).

CWDC (2009b) *Handbook for Candidates: A Guide to the Gateway Review and the Assessment Process*. Leeds: CWDC.

CWDC (2009c) *The Team Around the Child (TAC) and the Lead Professional: A Guide for Practitioners.* Leeds CWDC. Available online at: www.dcsf.gov.uk/everychildmatters/resources-and-practice/ IG00064 (accessed 6 March 2010).

Chilvers, D (2008) Follow me: planning to follow children's interests. *Nursery World,* 29 October: 18–21.

Chung, S and Walsh, DJ (2000) Unpacking child-centredness: a history of meanings. *Journal of Curriculum Studies,* 32(2): 215–234.

Clark, A (2010) Listening to children, in Miller, L, Cable, C and Goodliff, G (eds) *Supporting Children's Learning in the Early Years* (2nd edn). London: Routledge.

Clark, A and Moss, P (2005) *Spaces to Play: More Listening to Young Children Using the Mosaic Approach.* London: National Children's Bureau.

Clarke, J (2007) *Sustaining Shared Thinking.* London: Featherstone Education.

Cooke, T (1994) *So Much.* London: Walker Books.

Craft, A (2000) *Creativity Across the Primary Curriculum.* London: Routledge Flame.

Dahlberg, G, Moss, P and Pence, A (2006) *Beyond Quality in Early Childhood Education and Care: Languages of Evaluation* (2nd edn). London: Routledge.

Dalli, C (2008) Pedagogy, knowledge and collaboration: towards a ground-up perspective on professionalism. *European Early Childhood Education Research Journal,* 16(2), June: 171–185.

David, T, Gooch, K, Powell, S and Abbott, L (2003) *Birth to Three Matters: A Review of Literature.* Nottingham: DfES Publications.

Department for Education and Science (DES) (1967) *Children and their Primary Schools: A Report of the Central Advisory Council for Education (England)* (The Plowden Report). London: HMSO.

DES (1990) *The Rumbold Report: Starting with Quality.* London: DES.

DfES (2004) *Every Child Matters: Change for Children.* Nottingham: DfES.

DfES (2006) *Early Support and You: A Guide to the Early Support Programme.* Nottingham: DCSF.

Department for Children, Schools and Families (DCSF) (2007a) *Confident, Capable and Creative: Supporting Boys' Achievements.* Nottingham: DCSF.

DCSF (2007b) *Supporting Children Learning English as an Additional Language.* Nottingham: DCSF.

DCSF (2008a) *Statutory Framework for the Early Years Foundation Stage.* Nottingham: DCSF.

DCSF (2008b) *The Children's Plan One Year On – A Progress Report.* Nottingham: DCSF.

DCSF (2008c) *Early Years Quality Improvement Support Programme (The National Strategies/Early Years).* Nottingham: DCSF.

DCSF (2008d) *Practice Guidance for the Early Years Foundation Stage.* Nottingham: DCSF.

DCSF (2008e) *Principles into Practice (PiP) Cards: Early Years Foundation Stage.* Nottingham: DCSF.

DCSF (2008f) *The Early Years Foundation Stage* (CD-ROM). Nottingham: DCSF.

DCSF (2008g) *2020: Children and Young People's Strategy*. Nottingham: DCSF.

DCSF (2008h) *Inclusion Development Programme – Supporting Children with Speech, Language and Communication Needs: Guidance for Practitioners Working in the Early Years Foundation Stage*. Nottingham: DCSF.

DCSF (2008i) *Social and Emotional Aspects of Development: Guidance for Practitioners Working in the Early Years Foundation Stage*. Nottingham: DCSF.

DCSF (2008j) *Mark Making Matters: Young Children Making Meaning in all Areas of Learning and Development*. Nottingham: DCSF.

DCSF (2008k) *Safer Children in a Digital World: The Report of the Byron Review*. Nottingham: DCSF.

DCSF (2008l) *Every Child a Talker: Guidance for Early Language Lead Practitioners*. Nottingham: DCSF.

DCSF (2009a) *Learning, Playing and Interacting – Good Practice in the Early Years Foundation Stage (The National Strategies/Early Years)*. Nottingham: DCSF.

DCSF (2009b) *Inclusion Development Programme – Supporting Children on the Autistic Spectrum: Guidance for Practitioners in the Early Years Foundation Stage*. Nottingham: DCSF.

DCSF (2009c) *Building Futures: Believing in Children – A Focus on Provision for Black Children in the Early Years Foundation Stage*. Nottingham: DCSF.

DCSF (2009d) *The Children's Plan Two Years On: A Progress Report*. Nottingham: DCSF.

DCSF (2009e) *Next Steps for Early Learning and Childcare: Building on the 10-year Strategy*. Nottingham: DCSF.

DCSF (2009f) *Breaking the Link Between Disadvantage and Low Attainment: Everyone's Business*. Nottingham: DCSF.

Desforges, C with Abouchaar, A (2003) *The Impact of Parental Involvement, Parental Support and Family Education on Pupil Achievements and Adjustment: A Literature Review*. London: DfES.

Devereux, J (2010) Observing children, In Miller, L, Cable, C and Goodliff, G (eds) *Supporting Children's Learning in the Early Years* (2nd edn). London: Routledge.

Dillon, J, Rickinson, M, Teamey, K, Morris, M, Young Choi, M, Sanders D and Benefield, P (2006) The value of outdoor learning: evidence from research in the UK and elsewhere. *School Science Review*, 87(320), March: 107–111.

Donaldson, M (1978) *Children' Minds*. London: Fontana.

Dowling, M (2010) Emotional well-being, in Miller, L, Cable, C and Goodliff, G (eds) *Supporting Children's Learning in the Early Years* (2nd edn). London: Routledge.

Drake, J (2009) *Planning for Children's Play and Learning: Meeting Children's Needs in the Later Stages of the EYFS* (3rd edn). London: Routledge.

Drummond, MJ (2010) Under the microscope, in Smidt, S (ed.) *Key Issues in Early Years Education* (2nd edn). London: Routledge.

Edwards, CP, Gandani, L and Forman, G (1998) *The Hundred Languages of Children: Reggio Emilia Approach – Advanced Reflections*. London: Ablex Publishing.

Egan, B (2009) Learning conversations and listening pedagogy: the relationship in student teachers' developing professional identities. *European Early Childhood Research Journal*, 17(1), March: 43–56.

Elfer, P, Goldschmied, E and Selleck, D (2003) *Key Persons in the Nursery: Building Relationships for Quality Provision*. London: David Fulton.

Elfer, P (2009) Safe, secure and happy? Promoting emotional well-being in young children in nursery. Keynote address at the Pre-school Learning Alliance Annual Conference, 19 June. Available online at: www.pre-school.org.uk/documents/589 (accessed 2 January 2010).

Evans, M (2008) Work Matters: EYS training Part 1 – a complex role. *Nursery World*, 15 October: 28–29.

Feinstein, L (2003) Inequality in early cognitive development of British children in the 1970 cohort. *Economica*, New Series, 70(277), February: 73–97.

Feinstein, L, Hearn, B and Renton, Z with Abrahams, C and MacLeod, M (2007) *Reducing Inequalities: Realising the Talents of All*. London: National Children's Bureau.

Fillipini, T and Vecchi, V (eds) (1997) *The Hundred Languages of Children: Narrative of the Possible*. Reggio Emilia, Italy: Reggio Children.

Fisher, J (2008) *Starting from the Child* (3rd edn). Maidenhead: OUP.

Fisher, R (2002) Creative minds: building communities of learning for the creative age. Paper presented at the Teaching Qualities Initiative Conference, Hong Kong Baptist University.

Frost, J (2010) *A History of Children's Play and Play Environments: Towards a Contemporary Child-saving Movement*. London: Routledge.

Gardner, H (1993) *Frames of Mind: The Theory of Multiple Intelligences* (2nd edn). London: Fontana Press.

Gardner, H (1999) *The Disciplined Mind: Beyond Facts and Standardised Tests, The K-12 Education that Every Child Deserves*. New York: Simon & Schuster.

Gill, T (2007) *No Fear: Growing Up in a Risk Averse Society*. London: Calouste Gulbenkian Foundation.

Glassman, WE and Hadad, M (2998) *Approaches to Psychology* (5th edn). Maidenhead: OUP/McGraw-Hill Education.

Goldschmied, E and Jackson, S (2004) *People Under Three: Young Children in Day Care* (2nd edn). London: Routledge.

Goleman, D (1996) *Emotional Intelligence: Why it Can Matter More than IQ*. London: Bloomsbury.

Grenier, J (1999) The great outdoors. *Nursery World*, 16 September: 12–13.

Grenier, J (2005) All about . . . developing positive relations with children. *Nursery World*, 2 June: 14–21.

Harms, T, Clifford, R and Cryer, D (1998) *Early Childhood Environment Rating Scale*. New York and London: Teachers' College Press.

Harms, T, Clifford, RM and Cryer, D (2004) *Early Childhood Environment Rating Scale, Revised Edition*. New York: Teachers' College Press.

High Scope Educational Research Foundation (2007) *Does the High Scope Approach Really Work?* Hebburn, Tyne and Wear: High Scope UK. Available online at: www.high-scope.org.uk/about_high scope/18.asp (accessed 7 January 2010).

Hohmann, M and Weikart, D (2002) *Educating Young Children* (2nd edn). Ypsilanti, MI: High Scope Press.

HM Treasury (2004) (on behalf of Her Majesty's Stationery Office) *Choice for Parents, the Best Start for Children: A Ten Year Strategy for Childcare*. London: HMSO.

Ingleby, E and Oliver, G (2008) *Applied Social Science for Early Years*. Exeter: Learning Matters.

Jackson, L (2005) Who are you calling a pedagogue? *Guardian*, 18 May.

James, A, Jenks, C and Prout, A (1998) *Theorizing Childhood*. Cambridge: Policy Press/Blackwell.

Johnston, J and Nahmad-Williams, L (2009) *Early Childhood Studies*. London: Pearson/Longman.

Jones, C (2004) *Supporting Inclusion in the Early Years*. London: Sage.

Katz, L (2010) A developmental approach to the curriculum in the Early Years, in Smidt, S (ed.) *Key Issues in Early Years Education* (2nd edn). London: Routledge.

Kornbeck, J (2002) Reflection on the exportability of social pedagogy and its possible limits. *Social Work in Europe*, 9(2): 37–49.

Knight, S (2009) *Forest Schools and Outdoor Learning in the Early Years*. London: Sage.

Laevers, F (1994) *The Leuven Involvement Scale for Young Children (LIS-YC)* (manual and video tape). Experiential Education Series No 1. Leuven, Belgium: Centre for Experiential Education, University of Leuven.

Laevers, F (2003) Experiential education: making care and education more effective through well-being and involvement, in Laevers, F and Heylen, L (eds) *Involvement of Children and Teacher Style: Insights from an International Study on Experiential Education*. Studia Pedagogica 35. Leuven: Leuven University Press: 13–24.

Laevers, F (2006) Making care and education more effective through well-being and involvement: an introduction to Experiential Education. Conference paper from Her Majesty's Inspectorate of Education Early Years Good Practice Conference, Edinburgh, May. Available online at: www.hmie.gov.uk/documents/publication/HMIEConf%20DynamicL2%20May06.pdf (accessed 22 February, 2010).

Laevers, F and Heylen, L (eds) (2003) *Involvement of Children and Teacher Style: Insights from an International Study on Experiential Education*. Leuven, Belgium: Leuven University Press.

Laevers, F (ed.) with Daems, M, De Bruyckere, G, Declerq, B, Moons, J, Silkens, K, Snoek, G and Van Kessel, M (2005) *Well-being and Adult Involvement in Care Settings. A Process-oriented Self-evaluation Instrument, A Manual*. Leuven, Belgium: Centre for Experiential Education, University of Leuven. Available online at: www.kindengezin.be/Images/ZikohandleidingENG_tcm149-50761.pdf (accessed 19 November 2009).

Lancaster, YP (2006) Listening to young children: respecting the voice of the child, in Pugh, G and Duffy, B (eds) *Contemporary Issues in the Early Years* (4th edn). London: Sage.

Lane, J (2008) *Young Children and Racial Justice: Taking Action for Racial Equality in the Early Years – Understanding the Past, Thinking About the Present, Planning for the Future*. London: National Children's Bureau.

Lave, J and Wenger, E (1991) *Situated Learning: Legitimate Peripheral Participation*. Cambridge: University of Cambridge Press.

Learning and Teaching Scotland (2005) *Let's Talk about Pedagogy: Towards a Shared Understanding for Early Years Education in Scotland*. Edinburgh: Scottish Executive/Learning and Teaching Scotland.

Lindon, J (1999) Run the risk. *Nursery World*, 23 September: 10–11.

Lindon, J (2006) *Equality in Early Childhood: Linking Theory and Practice*. London: Hodder Arnold.

Lindqvist, G (2001) When small children play: how adults dramatise and children create meaning. *Early Years*, 21(1): 7–14.

Long, M and Sato, C (1984) Methodological issues in interlanguage studies: an interactionist perspective, in Davies, A, Criper, C and Howatt, A (eds) *Interlanguage*. Edinburgh: Edinburgh University Press.

Malaguzzi (1993) For an education based on relationships. *Young Children*, November: 9– 13.

Manning-Morton, J and Thorp, M (2003) *Key Times for Play: The First Three Years*. Maidenhead: OUP.

Marsh, J and Hallet, E (2008) *Desirable Literacies: Approaches to Language and Literacy in the Early Years* (2nd edn). London: Sage.

Maslow, A (1999) *Toward a Psychology of Being* (3rd edn). New York: Wiley.

Massey, S (2005) The benefits of a Forest School experience for children in their early years. Research paper for Worcestershire LEA. Available online at: www.worcestershire.gov.uk/cms/pdf/Worcs%20Forest%20School%20Research%20Academic%20Journal.pdf (accessed 5 January 2010).

Mathers, S, Linskey, F, Seddon, J and Sylva, K (2007) Using quality rating scaled for professional development: experiences in the UK. *International Journal of Early Years Education*, 15(3), October: 261–274.

Matthews, J (1999) *The Art of Childhood and Adolescence: The Construction of Meaning*. London: Falmer Press.

Mayesky, M (1998) *Creative Art and Activities*. Andover: Cengage Learning.

McDermott, D (2008) *Developing Caring Relationships Among Parents, Children, Schools, and Communities*. London: Sage.

McGillivray, G (2008) Nannies, nursery nurses and Early Years professionals: constructions of professional identity in the Early Years workforce in England. *European Early Childhood Research Journal*, 16(2): 242–254.

McMillan, M (1930) *The Nursery School*. London: Dent.

McShane, J (2007) Pedagogy: what does it mean? *Teaching Expertise*. Available online at: www.teachingexpertise.com/articles/pedagogy-what-does-it-mean-2370 (accessed 1 November 2009).

Meade, A and Cubey, P (2008) *Thinking Children: Learning about Schemas*. Maidenhead: OUP.

Melhuish, EC (2004) *Child Benefits: The Importance of Investing in Quality Childcare*. London: Daycare Trust.

Miller, L, Cable, C and Goodliff, G (eds) (2010) *Supporting Children's Learning in the Early Years* (2nd edn). London: Routledge.

Montessori, M (1912) *The Montessori Method*. London: Heinemann.

Mortimore, P (ed.) (1999) *Understanding Pedagogy and its Impact on Learning*. London: Paul Chapman.

Moss, P (2000) Training and education of early childhood education and care staff. Report prepared for the Organisation for Economic Cooperation and Development (OECD). London: Thomas Coram Research Institute/Institute of Education, University of London.

Moss, P and Petrie, P (2002) *From Children's Services to Children's Spaces*. London: Taylor & Francis.

Moyles, J (2007) *Early Years Foundations Meeting the Challenge*. Maidenhead: OUP.

Moyles, J (2010) The powerful means of learning in the Early Years, in Smidt, S (ed.) *Key Issues in Early Years Education* (2nd edn). London: Routledge.

Moyles, J, Adams, S and Musgrove, A (2002a) *SPEEL: The Study of Pedagogical Effectiveness in Early Learning*. Research Report 363, London: DfES.

Moyles, J, Adams, S and Musgrove, A (2002b) *Study of Pedagogical Effectiveness in Early Learning (SPEEL)*, DfES Research Brief RB363. Available online at: http://publications.dcsf.gov.uk/default.aspx?PageFunction =productdetails&PageMode=publications&ProductId=RR363& (accessed 12 November 2009).

New Zealand Ministry of Education (NZME) (1996) *Te Whāriki: Early Childhood Curriculum Policy Statement*. Wellington, NZ: NZME. Available online at: www.educate.ece.govt.nz/learning/curriculum AndLearning/TeWhariki.aspx (accessed 30 October 2009).

NZME (2002) *Pathways to the Future – Ngā Huarahi Arataki*. Wellingon, NZ: Learning Media.

Nutbrown, C (2006a) Watching and listening: the tools of assessment, in Pugh, G and Duffy, B (eds) *Contemporary Issues in the Early Years* (4th edn). London: Sage.

Nutbrown, C (2006b) *Threads of Thinking: Young Children Learning and the Role of Early Education* (3rd edn). London: Sage.

Nutbrown, C and Page, J (2008) *Working with Babies and Children: From Birth to Three*. London: Sage.

Ofsted (2008) *Leading to Excellence*. Available online at: http://www.ofsted.gov.uk/Ofsted-home/ Leading-to-excellence (accessed 12 February 2010).

Ofsted (n.d.) http://www.ofsted.gov.uk/ (accessed 12 February 2010).

Oldfield, L (2001) *Free to Learn: Introducing Steiner Waldorf Education*. Stroud: Hawthorn Press.

Osgood, J (2006) Deconstructing professionalism in early childhood education: resisting the regulatory gaze. *Contemporary Issues in Early Childhood*, 7(1): 5–14.

Ouvry, M (2003) *Exercising Muscles and Minds: Outdoor Play and the Early Years Curriculum*. London: National Children's Bureau.

Pakai, E (2004) Te Whāriki: the curriculum for early childhood education in Aotearoa/New Zealand. Paper presented to REACH, Victoria University, Canada, 25 June. Available online at: http://reach. uvic.ca/PPT/Pakai_paper.pdf (accessed 2 January 2010).

Palaiologou, I (2008) *Childhood Observation*. Exeter: Learning Matters.

Papatheodorou, T (2004) *Review: Assessing Quality in the Early Years. Early Childhood Environment Rating Scale (ECERS-E) Four Curricula Subscales*. Available online at: http://escalate.ac.uk/169 (accessed 25 February 2010).

Papatheodorou, T (2006) Seeing the wider picture: reflections on the Reggio Emilia approach. Paper reflecting on Early Years issues, available from Training, Advancement and Cooperation in Teaching

Young Children (TACTYC), online at: www.tactyc.org.uk/pdfs/Reflection_Papatheodorou.pdf (accessed 19 December 2009).

Parker-Rees, R (2007) Liking to be liked: imitation, familiarity and pedagogy in the first year of Life. *Early Years*, 27(1): 3–17.

Pascal, C and Bertram, A (2000) *The Effective Early Learning Project: Achievements and Reflections*. London: House of Commons, Available online at: www.publications.parliament.uk/pa/cm199900/cmselect/cmeduemp/386/0061406.htm (accessed 20 November 2009).

Pascal, C and Bertram, T (2001) *Effective Early Learning: Case Studies in Improvement*. London: Paul Chapman.

Pascal, C, Bertram, A, Ramsden, F, Georgeson, J, Saunders, M and Mould, C (1996) *Evaluating and Developing Quality in Early Childhood Settings: A Professional Development Programme*. Worcester: Amber Publications.

Pavlov, IP (1927). *Conditioned Reflexes: An Investigation of the Physiological Activity of the Cerebral Cortex* (trans. Anrep, GV). Oxford: Oxford University Press.

Penn, H (2008) *Understanding Childhood: Issues and Controversies* (2nd edn). Maidenhead: OUP.

Pere, RT (1983) *Ako*: concepts and learning in the Māori tradition. Working paper no. 17. Hamilton, New Zealand: University of Waikato.

Petrie, P (2005) Extending 'pedagogy'. *Journal of Education for Teaching*, 31(4): 293–296.

Petrie, P, Boddy, J, Cameron, C, Heptinstall, E, McQuali, S, Simon, A and Wigfall, V (2005) Pedagogy – a holistic, personal approach to work with children and young people across services. Briefing paper, June. Available online at: www.ncb.org.uk/dotpdf/open_access_2/cwc_handout2_pedagogy_paper.pdf (accessed 29 December 2009).

Piaget, J (1952) *The Child's Conception of Number*. New York: Humanities Press.

Piaget, J and Inhelder, B (1969) *The Psychology of the Child*. New York: Basic Books.

Pottier, J (1997) Towards an ethnography of participatory appraisal, in Grillo, RD and Stirrat, RL (eds) *Discourses of Development: Anthropological Perspectives*. Oxford: Berg.

Pugmire-Stoy, M (1992) *Spontaneous Play in Early Childhood*. Florence, KY: Delmar.

Qualifications and Curriculum Authority (QCA) (2000) *Curriculum Guidance for the Foundation Stage*. London: QCA/DfEE.

QCA/DCSF (2008) *Early Years Foundation Stage Profile Handbook and Assessment Scales Reference Sheet*. London: National Assessment Agency.

Rinaldi, C (2001) A pedagogy of listening: a perspective of listening from Reggio Emilia. *Children in Scotland*, September: 2–5.

Rinaldi, C (2006) *In Dialogue with Reggio Emilia: Listening, Researching and Learning*. London: Routledge.

Ring, K (2001) Young children drawing: the significance of the context. Paper presented at the British Educational Research Association Annual Conference, University of Leeds, 13–15 September. Available online at: www.leeds.ac.uk/educol/documents/00001927.htm (accessed 12 January 2010).

Robson, S (2010) The physical environment, in Miller, L, Cable, C and Goodliff, G (eds) *Supporting Children's Learning in the Early Years* (2nd edn). London: Routledge.

Rogoff, B (1990) *Apprenticeship in Thinking: Cognitive Development in Social Context*. New York: Oxford University Press.

Rogoff, B (2003) *The Cultural Nature of Human Development*. Oxford: Oxford University Press.

Roopnarine, I and Johnson, R (1987) *Approaches to Early Childhood Education*. Columbus. OH: Merrill Publishing.

Sammons, P, Taggart, B, Smees, R, Sylva, K, Melhuish, E, Siraj-Blatchford, I and Elliot, K (2003) *The Early Years Transition and Special Educational Needs (EYTSEN) Project*, DfES Research Brief RB431. Available from DCSF, online at: www.dcsf.gov.uk/research/data/uploadfiles/RB431.pdf (accessed 21 December 2009).

Sayeed, Z and Guerin, E (2000) *Early Years Play: A Happy Medium for Assessment and Intervention*. London: David Fulton.

Schaffer, HR and Emerson, PF (1964) The development of social attachment in infancy. *Monograph of the Society for Research in Child Development*, 29 (Serial No. 94).

Schaffer, HR (1996) Joint involvement episodes as contexts for development, in Daniels, H (ed.) *An Introduction to Vygotsky*. London: Routledge.

Schön, DA (1983) *The Reflective Practitioner: How Professionals Think in Action*. New York, NY: Basic Books.

Schweinhart, LJ (2000) The High Scope/Perry Pre-School Study: a case study in random assignment. *Evaluation and Research in Education*, 14(3/4): 136–147.

Siraj-Blatchford, I (2005) Quality interactions in the Early Years. Keynote address at the TACTYC Annual Conference, Cardiff, 5 November – Birth to 8 Matters! Seeking Seamlessness – Continuity? Integration? Creativity? Available online at: www.tactyc.org.uk/pdfs/2005conf_siraj.pdf (accessed 7 January 2010).

Siraj-Blatchford, I (2006) Diversity, inclusion and learning in the Early Years, in Pugh, G and Duffy, B (eds) *Contemporary Issues in the Early Years* (4th edn). London: Sage.

Siraj-Blatchford, I and Manni, L (2007) *Effective Leadership in the Early Years Sector: The ELEYS Study*. London: Institute of Education, University of London.

Siraj-Blatchford, I and Sylva, K (2004) Researching pedagogy in English pre-schools. *British Educational Research Journal*, 30(5): 713–730.

Siraj-Blatchford, I, Sylva, K, Muttock, S, Gilden, R and Bell, D (2002a) *Researching Effective Pedagogy in the Early Years (REPEY)*, DfES Research Report RR356. Norwich: DfES/HMSO. Available online at: www.dcsf.gov.uk/research/data/uploadfiles/RR356.pdf (accessed 3 December 2009).

Siraj-Blatchford, I, Sylva, K, Muttock, S, Gilden, R and Bell, D (2002b) *Researching Effective Pedagogy in the Early Years (REPEY)*, DfES Research Brief RB356. Available from DCFS, online at: www.dcsf.gov.uk/research/data/uploadfiles/RB356.pdf (accessed 21 December 2009).

Slater, L (2004) *Opening Skinner's Box: Great Psychological Experiments of the Twentieth Century*. London: Bloomsbury.

Smidt, S (2009) *Planning for the Early Years Foundation Stage*. London: Routledge.

Smith, AB (1988) Education and care components in New Zealand childcare centres and kindergartens. *Australian Journal of Early Childhood*, 13(3): 31–36.

Smith, LG and Smith, JK (1994) *Lives in Education: A Narrative of People and Ideas* (2nd edn). New York: St Martin's Press.

Smith, M (2008) Howard Gardner: multiple intelligences and education. *The Encyclopaedia of Informal Education (infed)*. Available online at: www.infed.org/thinkers/gardner.htm (accessed 3 January 2010).

Smith, M (2009) Donald Schön: learning, reflection and change. *The Encyclopaedia of Informal Education (infed)*. Available online at: www.infed.org/thinkers/et-schon.htm (accessed 9 January 2010).

Stephen, C (2006) *Early Years Education: Perspectives from a Review of the International Literature*. Available from the Scottish Executive, online at: www.scotland.gov.uk/Resource/Doc/92395/0022116.pdf (accessed 20 November 2009).

Stephen, C (2010) Pedagogy: the silent partner in Early Years learning. *Early Years*, 30(1): 1–14.

Stroh, K, Robinson, T and Proctor, A (2008) *Every Child Can Learn*. London: Sage.

Sylva, K, Siraj-Blatchford, I and Taggart, B (2004) *Assessing Quality in the Early Years: Early Childhood Environment Rating Scale (ECERS-E)* (2nd edn). Stoke-on-Trent: Trentham Books.

Sylva, K, Stein, A, Leach, P (2005) *Families, Children and Child Care Study*. Available online at: www.familieschildrenchildcare.org/fccc_frames_home.html (accessed 3 January 2010).

Sylva, K, Melhuish, E, Sammons, P, Siraj-Blatchford, I, Taggart, B and Elliot, K (2003) *The Effective Provision of Pre-School Education (EPPE) Project: Findings from the Pre-School Period*, DFES Research Brief RBX15-03. Available from Institute of Education, University of London, online at: http://eppe.ioe.ac.uk/eppe/eppepdfs/RB%20summary%20findings%20from%20Preschool.pdf (accessed 12 November 2009).

Sylva, K, Siraj-Blatchford, I, Taggart, B, Sammons, P, Melhuish, E, Elliot, K and Totsika, V (2006) Capturing quality in early childhood through environmental rating scales. *Early Childhood Research Quarterly*, 21: 76–92.

Sylva, K, Melhuish, E, Sammons, P, Siraj-Blatchford, I and Taggart, B (2010) *Early Childhood Matters: Evidence from the Effective Pre-School and Primary Education Project*. London: Routledge.

Thornton, L and Brunton, P (2009) *Understanding the Reggio Approach*. London: David Fulton.

Tovey, H (2007) *Playing Outdoors: Spaces and Places, Risks and Challenge*. Milton Keynes: OUP.

Tovey, H (2008) The dangers of safety: risk and challenge in play outdoors. Play Colloquium paper, Leeds: LMU.

Training Advancement and Cooperation in Teaching Young Children (TACTYC) (2005) How do we support children's sustained shared thinking? Paper from TACTYC Annual Conference, 5 November. Available online at: www.earlychildhoodaustralia.org.au/pdf/shared_thinking.pdf (accessed 4 December 2009).

Trevarthen, C (2001) Intrinsic motives for companionship in understanding their origin, development and significance for mental health. *Infant Mental Health Journal*, 22(1–2): 95–131.

United Nations (1989) *Convention on the Rights of the Child*. Available online at: www2.ohchr.org/english/law/crc.htm (accessed 3 January 2010).

Usher, R, Bryant, I and Johnson, R (1997) *Adult Education and the Postmodern Challenge: Learning Beyond the Limits*. London: Routledge.

Valentine, M (2006) *The Reggio Approach to Early Years Education*. Dundee: Scottish Consultative Council on the Curriculum.

Van Keulen, A (ed.) (2004) *Young Children Aren't Biased Are They? How to Handle Diversity in Early Childhood Education and School*. Amsterdam: SWP.

Vygotsky, L (1978) *Mind and Society*. Cambridge, MA: Harvard University Press.

Vygotsky, L (ed. Alex Kozulin) (1986) *Thought and Language*. London: MIT Press.

Vygotsky, L and Cole, M (eds) (1978) *Mind in Society: The Development of Higher Psychological Processes*. Cambridge, MA: Harvard University Press.

Wells, G (1985) *Language, Learning and Education*. Windsor: NFER/Nelson.

Wells, G (1987) *The Meaning Makers: Children Learning Language and Using Language to Learn*. London: Hodder & Stoughton.

Whalley, M and the Pen Green Team (2007) *Involving Parents in their Children's Learning* (2nd edn). London: Sage.

Whalley, ME, Allen, SF and Wilson, D (2008) *Leading Practice in Early Years Settings*. Exeter: Learning Matters.

Wheeler, H and Connor, J, with additional material by Goodwin, H (2009) *Parents, Early Years and Learning: Parents as Partners in the Early Years Foundation Stage – Principles into Practice*. London: National Children's Bureau

Willan, J (2009) Susan Isaacs – a modern educator for the 21st century. *Early Years Education*, 17 (2): 151–165.

Wood, E (2008) Conceptualising a pedagogy of play: international perspectives from theory, policy and practice, in Kuschner, D (ed.) *From Children to Red Hatters: Diverse Images and Issues of Play; Play and Culture Studies, Vol. 8*. Ablex, Maryland: University of America Press.

Wood, E and Attfield, J (2005) *Play, Learning and the Early Childhood Curriculum*. London: Paul Chapman.

Index

Abbott, L 9–10
Abouchaar, A 61
accommodation 147
active learning 30, 31*t*, 139
adult role 7–8, 134
adult–child interactions 16, 90–3, 91*t*, 102
Ainsworth, MDS 17
Anning, A 44
assessment 5, 31*t*, 34–5
 Common Assessment Framework 51–2
 documentation 76–7
 ECERS-E 123–4, 124*t*
 EYFS Profile 117–22
 EYQISP 124–6
 OFSTED 122–3
assimilation 147
Atherton, JS 146, 147
Athey, C 5, 35, 107
attachment theory 8, 17, 60, 85
Attfield, J 30, 35, 40–1, 44
autistic spectrum 47, 73, 80
autonomy 90, 94

Ball, C 9
Bandura, A 9, 17
Bee, H 27
behaviourism 16–17
Bell, SM 17
Bertram, A 8, 90, 93, 126
bilingualism 54
bodily–kinaesthetic intelligence 18
Bottle, G 40
Bowlby, J 8, 17
Boyd, D 27
brain development 26–7, 38, 53
British Educational Research Association (BERA) 25
Broadhead, P 30
Brodie, K 143
Bronfenbrenner, U 18–19
Brooker, L 77
Bruner, J 9, 17, 88, 100

Brunton, P 134
Byron Review 78

CAF (Common Assessment Framework) 51–2
Cahir, P 138
Cameron, C 14
Carr, M 101
child-centredness 25
child development 38–40
 brain development 26–7, 38, 53
 cognitive development 16, 17, 100, 102, 146
 holistic development 136
 stages of development 39, 146
 theories 16–20, 38
 see also Learning and Development
childcare 27, 132
childminding 85, 95, 133, 141
Children's Workforce 24, 51, 132
Children's Workforce Development Council (CWDC) 37, 43, 51 *see also* Standards
Chilvers, D 100
Chung, S 25
Clark, A 5, 6, 38, 106
Clarke, J 103
co-construction of meaning and learning 100, 102, 106–7
Code of Conduct 127–9, 128*t*
cognitive development 16, 17, 100, 102, 146
collaboration and co-operation 41, 46, 51
commitments 30, 31–2*t*
Common Assessment Framework (CAF) 51–2
communication, language and literacy (CLL) 16, 41–3, 42, 56–7, 107–9, 118 *see also* adult–child interactions
community of learners 140–2
competency (of children) 71–2
confidence 71–2
Connor, J 64
consistency 139
context 32*t*, 40–1, 136

continuing professional developoment 10–11
    community of learners 140–2
    Early Years Professional Networks 143–4
    effective pedagogy 131–3
    global influences 133–40
    inspiring others 144–5
convergent thinking 101
Cooke, T 57
Craft, A 100
creativity 32t, 35–7, 100
critical thinking 32t, 35–7
Cubey, P 35
curriculum 13, 40, 119, 134, 139
CWDC see Children's Workforce Development
    Council

Dahlberg, G et al. 10
Dalli, C 135
deep learning 89, 100
Denmark 24, 137–8
Department for Children, Schools and Families
    (DCSF)
    (2007a) 41
    (2007b) 54
    (2008a) 6, 29, 34, 46, 69, 84, 119
    (2008b) 1, 37
    (2008c) 2, 124–6
    (2008d) 3, 6, 7, 29, 30, 37, 39, 45, 67, 68f,
    78–9
    (2008e) (see Principles into Practice (PiP)
    cards)
    (2008f) 3
    (2008g) 29, 47, 51
    (2008h) 51, 54, 57
    (2008i) 54, 67
    (2008j) 77
    (2008k) 78
    (2008l) 118
    (2009a) 4, 35, 36, 38, 39, 40
    (2009b) 48, 69–70, 73
    (2009c) 57, 73
    (2009d) 60, 78, 115
    (2009e) 117
    (2009f) 116
Desforges, C 61
Devereux, J 33
Dewey, J 14
difference and diversity 6, 48–9

discovery learning 9
divergent thinking 101
documentation 76–7
Dowling, M 53
Drake, J 34
drawing 107–9
Drummond, MJ 34

EAL (English as an Additional Language) 54–6
Early Childhood Environmental Rating Scale
    Extension (ECERS-E) 10, 123–4, 124t
Early Years Foundation Stage (EYFS) 2, 29–34
    themes, principles and commitments 30,
    31–2t
Early Years Foundation Stage Profile (EYFS
    Profile) 117–22
Early Years Professional Networks 10–11,
    143–4
Early Years Professional Status (EYPS) 1, 37
Early Years Professionals (EYP)
    adult–child interactions 90–3, 91t, 102
    enablers and facilitators 88–9
    role 1, 29, 34, 83–96, 132
    see also key person (KP) role; leadership
Early Years Quality Improvement Support
    Programme (EYQISP) 2, 124–6
Early Years Transition and Special Educational
    Needs (EYTSEN) project 21–2, 23–4
ECERS-E see Early Childhood Environmental
    Rating Scale Extension
ecological systems theory 18–19
edu-care 10
Edwards, A 44
Edwards, CP et al. 5
Effective Early Learning (EEL) Project 8, 90, 93,
    126
Effective Leadership in Early Years Settings
    (ELEYS) 10
effective practice 2–3, 83–4, 115–18, 131–3
    see also evaluating effectiveness;
    Standards
Effective Provision of Pre-school Education
    (EPPE) project 20, 21, 22, 123, 139
Egan, B 105
Elfer, P et al. 8, 52, 87, 115
Emerson, PF 17
emotional environment 7, 75, 76
emotional intelligence 7, 59

emotional well-being 53–4
empathy 60
empowerment 136
Enabling Environments 7, 36, 72–4
  challenge 73
  commitments 31–2t, 72–3
  competency 71–2
  developing the environment 78–81
  emotional environment 7, 75, 76
  indoors 75–6
  learning environment 7, 32t, 70–1, 75–8,
    135
  outdoors 70–1, 75–6, 95, 138
  principle 31t
  safe and stimulating 7, 67–72, 68f
  sensory environment 73
  see also assessment; context; observation;
    planning; supporting learning
English as an Additional Language (EAL) 54–6
environment see Enabling Environments
EPPE project see Effective Provision of Pre-
    school Education
equality 6, 46–50
equilibration 147
evaluating effectiveness 114–30
  ECERS-E 123–4, 124t
  EYFS Profile 117–22
  EYQISP 124–6
  importance of Early Years provision 115–18
  OFSTED 122–3
  professional behaviour 127–9, 128t
Evans, M 84, 86–7
Every Child Matters 51, 52, 67
exosystem 18
Experiential Education (EXE) 89
EYFS see Early Years Foundation Stage
EYFS Profile (Early Years Foundation Stage
    Profile) 117–22
EYP see Early Years Professionals
EYPS (Early Years Professional Status) 1, 37
EYQISP (Early Years Quality Improvement
    Support Programme) 2, 124–6
EYTSEN project see Early Years Transition and
    Special Educational Needs

Family, Children and Child Care (FCCC) project
    27
Feinstein, L et al. 116

Fillipini, T 106, 107, 134
Fisher, J 42
Fisher, R 100
Forest Schools 137–8, 144
Foundation Stage Profile (FSP) see Early Years
    Foundation Stage Profile
Framework for Effective Pedagogy in the Early
    Years 21
Froebel, F 14
Frost, J 70

Gardner, H 17–18
Gill, T 66
Glassman, WE 17
Goldschmied, E 79–80, 84
Goleman, D 7
Gopnik, A et al. 38
Grenier, J 87, 137
guided participation 16, 100

Hallet, E 55, 56
Harms, T et al. 123
health and well-being 32t, 53–4
heuristic play 80–1
Heylen, L 8
High Scope 138–40
Hohmann, M 139
holistic development 136
home visits 52, 85–6
'Hundred Languages of Children' 5, 134

Inclusion Co-ordinators (INCOs) see
    SENCOs
inclusive practice 31t, 45–50
independence 39–40, 72, 75
integrated pedagogical model 93–6, 94f
integrated working 51–2
interactional learning 90–3, 91t
internet 77–8
interpersonal intelligence 18
intrapersonal intelligence 18
Isaacs, S 15

Jackson, S 79–80, 84
Johnson, R 14
Johnston, J 14, 16, 134
joint involvement episodes 100
Jones, C 48

Katz, L 37
key person (KP) role 8, 17, 32*t*, 52, 67, 84–7
Knight, S 69, 137
Kornbeck, J 24

Laevers, F 8, 89–90
Lancaster, YP 38
Lane, J 47
language *see* communication, language and
    literacy (CLL)
LAs (local authorities) 118
Lave, J 9, 100
Lead Professionals 51–2
leadership 2, 3, 6, 10, 11–12, 109–12
Learning and Development 4–6, 15–20,
    29–44
  absorption in learning 89–90
  active learning 30, 31*t*, 139
  areas 41*t*, 42
  co-construction of meaning and learning
    100, 102, 106–7
  commitments 31–2*t*
  context 40–1
  deep learning 89, 100
  discovery learning 9
  dispositions for learning 101
  integrated pedagogical model 93–6, 94*f*
  interactional learning 90–3, 91*t*
  learning outcomes 9
  learning processes 9
  observation, assessment and planning
    34–5
  principle 31*t*
  quality learning 9
  situated learning 9, 100
  supporting learning 31*t*, 32*t*, 34–6, 37
  'teacher' style 90
  see also adult–child interactions; child
    development; communication, language
    and literacy (CLL); creativity; critical
    thinking; play and exploration
Learning and Teaching Scotland 27
learning environment 7, 32*t*, 70–1, 75–8,
    135
Leuven Involvement Scale 89–90
Lindon, J 6, 137
Lindqvist, G 108
linguistic intelligence 18

listening to children 5, 38, 105–7
local authorities (LAs) 118
Locke, J 16
logical-mathematical intelligence 18
Long, M 88

McDermott, D 60–1
McGillivray, G 27, 132
McMillan, M 14–15
McMillan, R 14–15
macrosystem 18
McShane, J. 4
Makaton 47, 48, 75
Malaguzzi, L 5, 106, 107, 134
Manni, L 10, 127, 140
Manning-Morton, J 34
mark making 42, 107–9
Marsh, J 55, 56
Maslow, A 6
Massey, S 137
Mathers, S *et al.* 123
Matthews, J 107
Mayesky, M 100–1
Meade, A 35
mesosystem 18
microsystem 18
Montessori, M 14
Mortimore, P 13
Mosaic Approach 5, 38, 106–7
Moss, P 5, 6, 38, 106
Moyles, J *et al.* 4, 21, 23, 24, 30, 33, 38, 119
multiple intelligences 17–18
musical intelligence 18

Nahmad-Williams, L 14, 16, 134
networks 10, 11, 143–4
New Zealand 44, 101, 135
Nutbrown, C 34–5, 38

observation 5, 31*t*, 34–5, 88
Ofsted (Office for Standards in Education) 9,
    72, 122–3
Ouvry, M 70

Page, J 34–5
Pakai, E 136
Palaiologou, I 15, 133
Papatheodorou, T 123, 134

parents as partners 31t, 46, 60–4, 73–4, 76
    and EYFS Profile 118
    home visits 52, 85–6
    supporting learning and development
        115–17, 135
Parker-Rees, R 105
participatory appraisal 106
Pascal, C 8, 90, 93, 126
Pavlov, IP 16
pedagogy
    definitions 4, 13–14, 27
    effectiveness 131–3
    global influences 133–40
    integrated pedagogical model 93–6, 94f
    research studies 20–4, 26–7
    social pedagogues 24–5
    theoretical influences 14–15
Pen Green Loop 60, 61f
Penn, H 38, 71
Pere, RT 134
persona dolls 58–60
personal initiative 139
Pestalozzi, JH 14
Petrie, P et al. 25, 133
photographs 77
Piaget, J 16, 17, 146, 147
PiP cards see Principles into Practice (PiP)
    cards
plan–do–review 139, 140
planning 31t, 34–5
play and exploration 5, 16, 25–6, 30, 31t, 33,
        40–1
    and EYFS Profile 119
    heuristic play 80–1
    outdoor play 70–1, 95
    role play 68
Plowden Report 73
policy 46, 47, 48, 115, 117, 118
Positive Relationships 7–8, 31–2t, 36, 45–6,
        52–6, 136, 139 see also key person (KP)
        role; parents as partners; respecting each
        other; supporting learning
principles 30, 31t, 114
Principles into Practice (PiP) cards 3, 30,
        31–2t, 37, 40–1, 46, 47, 52, 72–3, 84,
        135
professional behaviour 127–9, 128t
Pugmire-Stoy, M 33

quality 3, 9–10
    assurance 9, 119–22
    improvement 9
    provision 9, 115
    regulation 9, 122–3
quality learning 9

reflection-in-action 104
reflection-on-action 104, 105
reflective practice 10–11, 41, 94, 103–5, 120,
        142
Reggio Emilia pre-schools 5, 34, 73, 76–7, 106,
        107, 134–5
relationships see Positive Relationships
Researching Effective Pedagogy in the Early
        Years (REPEY) project 4, 8, 21, 23, 99–100,
        102–3
resources 30, 46, 58–60, 67, 80
respecting each other 31t, 38, 136
Rinaldi, C 76, 106
Ring, K 107
risk 66, 67, 69–70
Robson, S 70
Rodger, R 9–10
Rogoff, B 16, 100
role play 68
Roopnarine, I 14
Rousseau, J-J 14
Rumbold Report 9

safety 32t, 67–72, 68f
Sammons, P et al. 21–2, 23–4
Sato, C 88
scaffolding 17, 88–9, 94, 100
Schaffer, HR 17, 100
schemas (schemes) 5, 35, 107, 147
schematic development 147
Schön, DA 103–4
self-esteem 55
self-identity 55
SENCOs (Special Educational Needs
        Co-ordinators) 50–1
SENs see special educational needs
sensitivity 90
sensory environment 73
Siraj-Blatchford, I et al. 4, 8, 10, 21, 23, 25, 55,
        88, 99–100, 102–3, 109, 111, 127, 140
situated learning 9, 100

Skinner, BF 16
Smidt, S 57, 119
Smith, AB 10
Smith, M 18, 104
social interaction 16, 88, 100
social learning theory 9, 17
social pedagogues 24–5
socio-cultural context 133–4
spatial intelligence 18
special educational needs (SENs) 22, 47–51,
    73–4
Special Educational Needs Co-ordinators
    (SENCOs) 50–1
SPEEL project see Study of Pedagogical
    Effectiveness in Early Learning
staff training
    key person (KP) approach 85, 86, 87
    sustained shared thinking 109–12
Standards 2, 35–7, 42–3
    1: 13, 14, 19, 34, 43, 114
    2: 5, 13, 14, 16, 19, 38, 94
    3: 19, 72
    4: 46
    5: 19, 46
    6: 46
    7: 2, 6, 25, 38, 47, 71, 83, 96, 140
    8: 2, 7, 73, 140
    9: 2, 6, 79, 94
    10: 2, 19, 34, 94, 140
    11: 2, 6, 74, 90, 94, 140
    12: 2, 6, 43, 46, 58, 67, 94
    13: 2, 94, 140
    14: 2, 89, 90, 94
    15: 2, 57
    16: 2, 8, 9, 30, 43, 89, 98
    17: 2, 19
    18: 2, 6, 46–7, 70, 94, 111
    19: 2, 6, 67, 69, 70, 78
    20: 2
    21: 2, 35, 94
    22: 2, 90, 140
    23: 2, 19, 50, 90
    24: 2, 38, 83, 96, 115
    25: 43, 45, 52
    26: 94
    27: 5, 20, 38, 45, 90, 94, 105, 140
    28: 19
    29: 19, 76
    30: 46, 74, 76
    31: 116
    32: 51
    33: 41, 43, 46, 57, 127
    34: 57
    35: 46, 70
    36: 46, 51, 72
    37: 43
    38: 10, 13, 41, 47, 103, 115, 134
    39: 10, 13, 47, 103, 134
Steiner, R 15
Stephen, C 13, 25
stimulation 90
story 56–7
Stroh, K et al. 53
Study of Pedagogical Effectiveness in Early
    Learning (SPEEL) project 4, 21, 23
supporting learning 31t, 32t, 34–6, 37
    adult–child interactions 16, 90–3, 91t, 102
    integrated pedagogical model 93–6, 94t
    parents' role 115–17, 135
sustained shared thinking 8–9, 98–112
    and children's mark making 107–9
    definitions 99–100
    leading practice 109–12
    links with theory 100–2
    listening to children 105–7
    reflective practitice 103–5
    REPEY study 99–100, 102–3
Sylva, K et al. 10, 20, 21, 22, 25, 27, 123,
    124

Te Whāriki 101, 135–6
'teacher' style 90
technology 77–8
themes 30, 31–2t
thinking skills 32t, 35–7, 101 see also
    creativity; sustained shared thinking
Thornton, L 134
Thorp, M 34
Tovey, H 30, 69
Training Advancement and Cooperation in
    Teaching Young Children (TACTYC) 100,
    102, 109
transitions 52–3, 72, 87

UN Convention on the Rights of the Child
    (UNCRC) 38, 106

'Unique Child' 6, 31–2t, 36, 119 *see also* child
    development; health and well-being;
    inclusive practice; safety; special
    educational needs
Usher, R *et al.* 104

Vecchi, V 106, 107, 134
visual timetables 47, 48
Vygotsky, L 8–9, 16, 30, 100

Walsh, DJ 25
Weikart, D 138, 139
Wells, G 56, 99
Wenger, E 9, 100
Whalley, M *et al.* 2, 11, 61, 62f
Wheeler, H 64
Wood, E 30, 35, 40–1, 44, 93, 94f

zone of proximal development (ZPD) 16, 17